Gifted Hands

REVISED KIDS EDITION

Other books in the
Zonderkidz Biography Series

Beyond the Music: The Bono Story

Defender of Faith: The Mike Fisher Story

Driven by Faith: The Trevor Bayne Story

Gift of Peace: The Jimmy Carter Story

Heart of a Champion: The Dominique Dawes Story

Linspired: The Jeremy Lin Story

Man on a Mission: The David Hilmer Story

Prophet with Honor: The Billy Graham Story

Reaching New Heights: The Kelly Clark Story

Speed to Glory: The Cullen Jones Story

Also by Gregg Lewis and Deborah Shaw Lewis

The Admiral: The David Robinson Story

Gifted Hands

the Ben Carson Story

REVISED KIDS EDITION

Gregg Lewis
and Deborah Shaw Lewis

ZONDERKIDZ

Gifted Hands, Revised Kids Edition
Copyright © 2013 by Gregg Lewis and Deborah Shaw Lewis

Requests for information should be addressed to:
Zonderkidz, 3900 Sparks Drive, Grand Rapids, Michigan 49546

Library of Congress Cataloging-in-Publication Data

Lewis, Gregg, 1951–
    Gifted hands : the Ben Carson story / Gregg Lewis and Deborah Shaw Lewis.
      p.   cm.
    Rev. ed. of: Gifted hands. c2009.
     ISBN 978-0-310-73830-5 (softcover)
    1. Carson, Ben—Juvenile literature. 2. Neurosurgeons—United States—
Biography—Juvenile literature. 3. African American surgeons—Biography—
Juvenile literature. I. Lewis, Deborah Shaw, 1951- II. Lewis, Gregg, 1951- Gifted
hands. III. Title.
    RD592.9.C37L49 2009b
    617.4'8092—dc22   2009005778

Interior design: Beth Shagene
Cover design: Mark Veldheer
Cover photo: Hilary Schwab, Shutterstock
Interior composition: Greg Johnson/Textbook Perfect

Printed in the United States of America

15 16 17 18 19 20 21 22 /DCI/ 22 21 20 19 18 17 16 15 14 13 12 11 10 9 8 7

Table of Contents

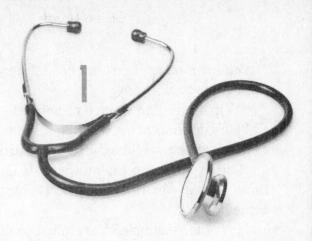

Broken Home, Shattered Dreams

For a long time, Ben had sensed that something was wrong. He had not heard his parents scream or shout at one another for days. He seldom even heard them argue. Instead they would just quit talking to each other until the whole house filled with a deep and disturbing quiet. Those silences gradually became longer and much more frequent. His father seemed to be gone more and more.

Yet Ben was still surprised by his mother's announcement.

It started like any other day for eight-year-old Ben Carson and his ten-year-old brother, Curtis. But it turned unforgettably sad when their mother sat them down and told them, "Boys, your father has moved out of this house. He's not going to be living with us anymore."

"I don't want him to leave!" Ben cried. "Please make him come back!"

But his mother shook her head. "Bennie, your father can't come back."

"Why not?" Ben wanted to know.

"He's done some ... some bad things." And that was as much as she would tell Ben and Curtis.

Ben argued with his mother. "If Daddy did something wrong, why can't you just forgive him and let him come home?"

"It's not that simple," she replied, looking like she was about to cry.

Ben wondered if he'd done something to make his father angry. But Ben's mother assured him that his daddy loved him very much and was not mad at him at all. Still, it hurt.

Ben's heart was broken. He loved his daddy. Every night he prayed for his father to come home so their family could be together again. But that never happened.

When he left, Ben's father took all of the family's money, including the "nest egg" Ben's mother had managed to store up by scrimping and saving over the years. Mrs. Carson had no job skills or work experience, so the only way she could support herself and her two sons was by cleaning houses and taking care of other people's children. It was hard work, but she was determined to do whatever it took to provide for her boys.

Even after he learned the truth, Ben continued to love his father in spite of what he had done. But Ben loved and respected his mother even more. He knew how hard she worked to take care of him and Curtis, and how much his father's actions had hurt his mother.

Sonya Carson, Ben's mother, had been born into a large and extremely poor rural Tennessee family. She was the next to the youngest of twenty-four children. Yet she only knew thirteen of her siblings because she spent most of her lonely and unhappy childhood moving from one foster home to another.

She had been just thirteen years old when she met and married Ben's father, an older man who promised to rescue her from her sad situation and take her north to Detroit. He promised to provide her with a life of wealth and adventure. Ben's father was a charming man and a good provider. He loved parties and seemed proud of his young wife. He often bought Ben's mother expensive gifts of clothing and jewelry. Ben's father seemed to spend money as fast as he earned it. Over time, Ben's mother became concerned about their finances.

After the boys were born, Ben's mother wondered where her husband was getting his extra money. She worried that he might be involved in selling alcohol or even drugs.

She finally found out that he had another wife and family, and Sonya told him to leave.

Ben found it tough to give up his hopes for a happy home where his family could all live together again. But the same year his father left, a new dream entered Ben's life.

That dream was born one Sunday morning during church. Ben sat on the edge of the pew, listening intently, as their minister told an exciting true story about a missionary doctor.

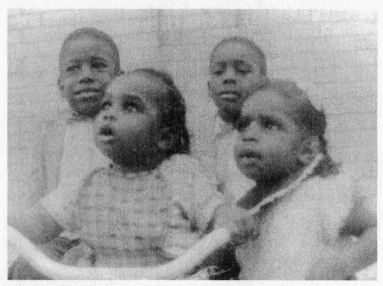

Ben and Curtis Carson (back row) with childhood friends.

"Robbers were chasing the doctor and his wife," the minister told them. "They ran as fast as they could around trees and over rocks, trying to stay ahead of their pursuers. Then they came to the edge of a cliff. They had nowhere to go. But right at the very brink of the precipice, they spotted a crack in the rock just big enough for both of them to crawl into.

"When the bandits got to the cliff, their would-be victims were nowhere to be seen. It was as if the doctor and his wife had vanished! The robbers didn't know what to think. They stomped around, cursing, then left. The missionaries were safe."

As the story ended, Ben breathed a sigh of relief. *What a thrilling life missionaries must lead!*

"God hid his missionaries in the cleft of the rock," the pastor explained. "And he will do the same for you if you give him your heart and let him protect you from harm."

That's what I need, thought Ben. So when the preacher invited those who wanted to give their lives to Jesus to come forward, Ben walked down the aisle to where the minister was standing. After listening to that exciting story, Ben knew two things: he wanted Jesus to watch over him, and he knew what he wanted to do with his life.

"I know what I will be when I grow up," Ben told his mother as they walked home from church that day, "a missionary doctor!"

His mother stopped to look right at him. "Bennie," she said, "if you ask the Lord for something and believe he will do it, it *will* happen."

His mother's encouraging response confirmed the dream for him. From that time on, Ben was convinced that God wanted him to be a doctor one day. Somehow he held on to that dream despite many other difficult things that would happen in his young life.

* * *

Since Ben's father was no longer providing any money, Sonya had to work longer and longer hours, holding two or three jobs at a time. Many mornings she left before dawn and wouldn't get home until her sons were already asleep. Sometimes two or three days would go by without Ben or Curtis even seeing their mother.

Her exhausting schedule, the pain and sadness she felt about the end of her marriage, the heavy responsibility of raising two boys alone, and her own fear and uncertainty about the future all added up to an overwhelming feeling of discouragement and depression. Sonya often worried she might not be strong enough to make it on her own. Sometimes she wasn't sure she could go on another day.

Eventually, a few months after Ben's father had left, Sonya decided she needed help. She told the boys, "I have to go away for a few days to see some relatives."

"Are we going too?" Ben wanted to know.

"No, Bennie," she said, "I have to do this alone. Besides, you boys need to go to school. So I've made arrangements for you." Sister Scott, an elderly woman they knew from church, stayed at their house and took care of Ben and Curtis. "Just until I come back," their mother told them.

Sonya made it sound like a special adventure. And the boys enjoyed spending time with Sister Scott. She was a terrific listener who would focus on whatever the boys told her and would exclaim, "Oh, my!" every other sentence or so.

One day Sister Scott found out that Ben and Curtis wanted to learn how to roller-skate. "I can teach you," she told them. And she strapped on a pair of old-fashioned, one-size-fits-all skates—the kind that fit onto one's shoes and are adjusted with a metal key. Then she gave the boys a demonstration.

They created a sensation in the neighborhood—an

eighty-year-old woman skating up and down the side-walks of Detroit with two boys in tow. Ben and Curtis had all they could do to keep up with her. They thought, *If an old lady like her can roller-skate, we can too!* And before long they could.

The boys never really wondered why their mother made a number of those "visits to relatives" over the next few months. Not until they were adults did Ben and Curtis learn that those special occasions when their mother went away were actually times she felt so overwhelmed by life that she would temporarily check herself into a mental hospital to get treatment for depression and emotional stress. Then, when she felt capable of coping with life again, she'd check out and her sons would welcome her home. Life would go on after each "trip."

Every summer included one day at the Michigan State Fair. Sonya would save just enough money to pay for their admission so Ben and Curtis could take in the arts and crafts, agriculture, livestock, and educational exhibits.

But they never had enough to pay for tickets to any of the midway rides. The boys could only watch other children on the rides and listen to the high-pitched screams as children were tossed and spun and whirled through the air. Ben especially liked watching children riding in the bumper cars, banging into each other and laughing. For years he dreamed of driving one himself and tried to imagine what that would be like.

Over time, Ben learned that he could find enjoyment by imagining many things. He had never flown on an airplane, or seen a luxury cruise ship, or been inside a limousine, or even eaten in a sit-down restaurant. But he learned that his imagination could create vivid pictures of what such experiences would be like.

* * *

Sonya Carson continued struggling to pay her bills and care for her sons. As the months passed, it became clear that there was no way they could afford to stay in their Detroit home. To save money, Ben's mother decided to move her little family to Boston, Massachusetts. They would live with her older sister and brother-in-law, Ben's Aunt Jean and Uncle William Avery. Sonya explained to the boys that they would rent out their house in Detroit for enough money to cover the monthly mortgage payments. That way, when times got better and she had saved enough money, they could move back into their home on Deacon Street.

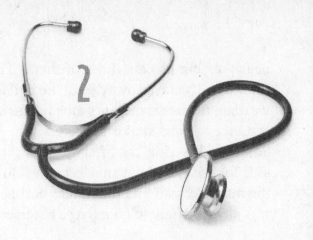

Beantown Rats, Spiders, and Change

Ben felt sad about leaving his home and friends in Michigan to live in a tenement building in Boston.

But it wasn't long before he found out there was definitely an upside to living with the Averys. Their children were grown, so they had lots of love to show two young boys. That first Christmas the Carsons lived in Boston, Ben's aunt, uncle, and mother showered the boys with gifts.

Ben's favorite present was a chemistry set. He spent hours in his room, reading the instructions, mixing chemicals, and watching them react. One of his experiments left the apartment smelling like rotten eggs. Ben thought that was hilarious.

Not everything about the move was positive, however.

Ben hated the rats that roamed in packs in the weeds behind the apartment building. Big rats. Ugly rodents

nearly as big as cats. Lots of them. The horrid creatures usually stayed away from the building. But in cold
weather, the rats sometimes took refuge in the basement.

Once, a big snake slithered into the basement.
Someone killed it, but afterward all the neighborhood
kids told stories about snakes eating children. Between
the rats he'd seen and the snakes he'd heard about, Ben
was always afraid to go into the basement.

* * *

When they did feel the need for outdoor adventure, Ben
and Curtis often played in a park not far from their apartment building. There they imagined their own mountain-
climbing and Wild West exploits as they scampered up,
over, and around the large rock formations.

One day, Ben climbed across the face of a rock wall
on a dangerously high and narrow ledge. With one hand
firmly jammed in a crack, he plastered his body against
the rock as tightly as he could, slowly easing himself
forward and feeling for someplace to hold on with his
other hand. Suddenly a chunk of ledge gave way beneath
his feet.

Ben was now dangling by just one hand. He listened
to the sound of the broken rock hitting the ground far
below.

He looked and, just an arm's length ahead, the remaining ledge looked wider and stronger. But how could
he get there? He needed a new handhold to reach it. From
where Ben hung, he spotted another crevice he thought

he could reach with his free hand. If he could get a good grip there, he could swing himself over to the ledge.

The trouble was, he could see a thick spider's web stretched across the opening.

Ben loved all kinds of animals. Well, *almost* all kinds of animals. He absolutely hated spiders. They terrified him. And he'd seen some humongous wolf spiders with webs just like this one among the rocks of that park. He thought, *There's no way I will stick my hand in that nest of wolf spiders!*

Then Ben looked down. He was a long way up. And the ground below was rocky. He did not want to think about how badly he'd be hurt if he fell from this height. He was terrified of spiders! But right then he was more afraid of falling.

I need a handhold in that crevice! Ben told himself. So he stretched and put his hand through the spider's web and into that opening in the rock. He gained a solid grip, swung his feet onto the ledge, and quickly scampered safely off that rock wall. Ben learned an important lesson: sometimes to survive you need to face your fear and overcome it.

The added sense of danger Ben experienced living in Boston wasn't merely the result of a young boy's fertile imagination. His new neighborhood was definitely tougher than the one he'd left in Detroit. He often encountered homeless drunks sleeping on the sidewalk outside his apartment building. All hours of the day, police cars raced through the streets — their sirens blasting, lights flashing.

One of the Averys' sons was shot to death on those streets. Ben had liked and looked up to that young adult cousin. But in addition to feeling a terrible sadness over his cousin's senseless death, Ben realized his cousin, by associating with drug dealers, had been doing something he shouldn't have been doing when he was killed.

That too was a valuable lesson. Ben made up his mind right then: *Some things aren't worth the risk.*

While the Carson family lived in Boston, Ben's mother made two or three more "visits to relatives" for three or four weeks at a time. But Ben and Curtis, though they missed their mother, never worried. They never questioned why she had to leave. They trusted Aunt Jean and Uncle William to take great care of them. Ben and Curtis were usually a bit spoiled by the time their mother returned.

In Boston, just as she had back in Detroit, Ben's mother worked for several well-to-do families, caring for their children or cleaning their houses. Many days she left for work early in the morning before her boys went to school and didn't get home until almost bedtime. Just the same, she always took time to ask Ben and Curtis what they were doing and learning in school — no matter how tired she was or how many hours she had worked that day.

Ben and his brother knew their mother thought their education was important and that she wanted them to excel in school. And they did. Both boys did well in their classes at the small private school they attended in Boston.

* * *

Ben's mother wanted her sons to learn the importance of setting goals in life. Almost every day, she talked to Ben and Curtis about her own goal of saving enough money to someday move back into their house in Detroit.

Sonya Carson also taught her sons the value of a dollar. For instance, riding to school on the city bus cost twenty cents a day — the same price as a loaf of bread then. So Ben and Curtis rode their bikes to school, and the money they saved was used to buy groceries for the family.

Ben's mother liked to say, "A penny saved is a penny earned." The boys learned never to be late in returning a library book. They never walked past an alley without looking to see if they could spot a bottle they could turn in for a penny deposit. No amount of money was too small when it came to spending — or saving.

There were other important lessons Sonya managed to teach her sons. And Ben was reminded of one of them the day a store clerk made the mistake of giving him too much change. Instead of a one-dollar bill, she handed Ben a ten. Even before he walked out the door of the store, he realized the mistake and excitedly began to fantasize. *What can I do with* my *extra nine dollars?* But by the time he reached home, Ben had a knot in his stomach the size of the fist in which he still clutched the money. And he was no longer feeling so great about his "good fortune."

Ben recognized the feeling he was experiencing. It was guilt. He knew keeping the money wouldn't be honest. And honesty was an important principle he'd learned from his mother as well as at church.

Ben immediately turned around and walked back to the store, where he returned the ten-dollar bill to the clerk and explained what had happened. She gave him the correct change, and he strode out of the store nine dollars poorer but feeling on top of the world.

Recalling the incident years later, Ben would say, "That experience reinforced for me an even more important truth than the virtue of honesty. It reminded me that there is such a thing as right and wrong, and when you do what is right, based on the principles you believe in, the satisfaction that results is better than having money."

* * *

During their two years in Boston, the Carson family saved enough pennies, nickels, and dimes to move back to Michigan. They still couldn't afford to live in the little house on Deacon Street. But they were closer. And the boys were glad to be near their old friends.

However, a few weeks after they returned to school in Detroit, both Ben and Curtis realized they had a serious problem. In Boston they had been among the better students in their classes; in Detroit, they were behind their classmates. Ben understood so little of what his class was studying, he began to fear his dream of becoming a missionary doctor was drifting out of reach. He also began to believe what the other kids were saying about him.

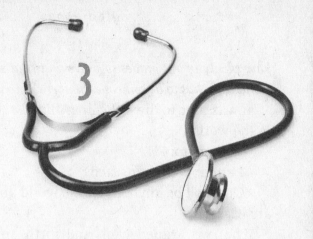

The Dumbest Kid in Fifth Grade

"Hey, Dummy!"

Ben looked up. "Dummy" was the nickname his new classmates had given him.

Another fifth grader laughed at Ben's instinctive response. "Ben Carson is *so* dumb."

Ben shrugged and tried to act as if he didn't mind. He didn't like being called dumb. Who would? But he figured what the students said was true. After all, he heard it every single day.

"Ben Carson's the dumbest kid in fifth grade!" the classmate continued.

Ben looked the other way. He wasn't in the mood to argue.

"Hey, Carson's the dumbest kid in the world!" someone else called out.

Now, wait a minute! Ben thought. *I know I'm dumb. I*

have plenty of test grades to prove that. But somewhere in the world there has to be someone dumber than me!

It was time to draw the line. "I'm *not* the dumbest kid in the world!"

"You are too!"

"I am not!" Ben insisted.

"Couldn't be anybody in the world dumber than you are, Carson!"

The two argued back and forth until the teacher called the class inside.

Later that same afternoon, there was a math quiz. Afterward, the teacher instructed each student to pass his test to the person behind him to correct as the teacher read out the answers. Ben knew what was coming next. Each student would have to report his or her score to the teacher — out loud!

Ben stared with disgust at the big fat zero at the top of his paper. *When everybody finds out what I made on this quiz*, he thought, *they'll never let up.*

That's when Ben began to scheme: *Maybe if I mumble*, he thought, *the teacher won't understand me.* So when the teacher called his name, he muttered, "Nnnme." And it worked!

"Nine? Benjamin! How wonderful! Class, can you see what Benjamin has done? Didn't I tell you if you just applied yourself you could do it? I'm so proud of you!"

Nine right would have meant Ben had twenty-one wrong, but nine was still a lot better than his usual grade. That must have been why the teacher kept raving on ... at least until the girl who had graded Ben's paper decided to set the record straight.

"He said *none!*" she spouted. "You know, *none* — as in *not any!*"

After a short pause, a chorus of laughter broke out in the room. The teacher shook her head as she sat down in her chair. Ben wanted to disappear. But he couldn't. So he just grinned and tried to pretend the laughter didn't bother him.

* * *

Ben felt especially dumb when all the fifth-grade students at Higgins Elementary had their eyes tested. The boy ahead of Ben rattled off the letters and numbers with ease. When Ben's turn came, he squinted and tried, but he could not make out any of the letters except for the very top line.

He was so embarrassed. He couldn't even read an eye chart correctly. "No wonder the kids call me Dummy," he mumbled.

"Being able to read an eye chart has nothing to do with being smart or dumb," the nurse replied. "You just need glasses."

Shortly after, a doctor fitted Ben with glasses. "Your vision is so bad," the doctor said, "you almost qualify as handicapped."

Wearing glasses changed Ben's life. When he wore them to school, Ben couldn't believe the difference. He could actually read what the teacher wrote on the board— even from the back of the room!

* * *

A few weeks later, Ben received his midterm grade report. He was not surprised to see an F next to most of his subjects. His brother's report looked nearly the same way. When Ben got home, he dropped his grade card and his books on the table, hoping his mother wouldn't see the report until after he was in bed.

That didn't happen. "Bennie, is this your midterm report?" she asked, looking it over carefully.

"Yes, ma'am," Ben replied, "but it doesn't mean much."

"No, Bennie," she answered, "it means a lot! If you keep making grades like this, you'll spend the rest of your life sweeping floors in a factory. And that's not what God wants for you."

Sonya pulled Ben and Curtis close to her and looked right into their faces. "Boys, I don't know what to do. But God promises in the Bible to give wisdom to those who ask. So tonight I'm going to pray for wisdom. I'm going to ask God what I need to do to help you."

Ben and Curtis didn't know what to think about their mother's words. Had she gone off the deep end? Did she really think God was going to tell her how to help them get better grades?

Two days later, the boys found out God's answer to their mother's prayer, and they didn't like it. "God says we need to turn off the television," Sonya told her sons. "You may choose three TV shows to watch each week, but three times per week is it. You can use the extra time for reading."

The boys complained and tried to change her mind, but their mother wasn't finished. "You're also to write two book reports every week about what you read. Then you can present your reports out loud to me."

God's answer didn't seem very wise to Ben or Curtis. But they did what their mother said. They turned off the television, walked to the nearest branch of the Detroit Public Library, and checked out a stack of books.

Some people thought Ben's mother was being too hard on her sons. Several of her friends talked to her, telling her the boys needed more time to play outside. They warned her that Curtis and Ben would hate her for making them turn off the TV to read books and write reports.

But those people were wrong. Ben never hated his mother. Yes, he told her she was making them work too hard. But inside he knew she loved him and Curtis, and only wanted the best for them.

Anytime Ben and his brother complained about the TV restrictions, Sonya Carson firmly held her ground and insisted: "If you boys keep reading books, someday people will be watching you on television!"

That prediction seemed more than a little far-fetched to Ben. But he definitely believed his mother when she said if he tried, he could do anything he wanted to do.

Sonya was tough and demanding. One day while she was driving Ben somewhere, the traffic stopped suddenly and another vehicle bumped them from behind. Without even getting out to see how much damage he had caused, the man in the other car quickly drove away.

Ben's mom chased him all the way across Detroit before he finally gave up, pulled over, and got out to show Sonya his insurance information so that his coverage would pay for her car to be fixed.

Sonya Carson was just as tough and demanding with her sons. She had high expectations for Curtis and Ben, and she never let them forget it. She observed the lives and habits of the successful and wealthy people whose homes she cleaned every day. "They are no different from us," she told her sons. "Anything they can do, you can do. And if you really want to and you work hard, you can do it better."

On occasion Ben's mother drove the boys out to the neighborhoods where she worked. As they gawked at the huge houses, Mrs. Carson would tell her sons, "You two have a choice. I've told you about the people I work for out here. How I've noticed they don't watch much television. They have a lot of books and always seem to be reading and learning. They also work hard—first to get a good education and then they work even harder to become successful in their careers. Because they do all that, they can afford to drive nice cars, build these big houses, and live in this beautiful neighborhood."

Then she would continue: "You've probably noticed that where we live, many people sit around drinking a lot, spend hours every day watching television, and live month to month on government welfare checks. Most of them will never afford to live anywhere but old, run-down houses and apartment buildings in neighborhoods like ours. But now that you see and know the difference, you boys know you have a choice about how and where you will live your lives."

Ben remembers, "Because we'd always been poor and I'd always hated poverty, my mother's strategy worked well for me. Once I knew there was a way out, once I realized the person who would have the most to do with what happened to me and my life was me, I discovered I didn't worry or hate poverty nearly as much. Because I knew it was temporary, and I had a choice."

In Sonya's mind, education would be the key to her sons' success. When other parents questioned the demands she placed on Curtis and Ben, she would tell them, "Say what you want, but my boys are going to be something. They're going to be self-supporting and learn how to love other folks. And no matter what they decide to do, they're going to be the best in the world at it."

The boys were grateful their mother hadn't said *what* they had to read. That meant they were free to choose books that interested them. Ben loved animals. So he read all the animal books he could find, then moved on to plants and rocks.

The Carsons lived near railroad tracks. Soon, Ben found himself collecting rocks in little boxes and taking them home to look up in his library books. Before long, he could identify almost any rock he found. He was proud of himself, but he thought it wise not to mention his new hobby to anyone at school.

One day Mr. Jaeck, Ben's science teacher, walked into his fifth-grade classroom with a big, shiny black rock. He held it up and asked, "Can anyone tell me what this is?"

Ben waited for one of the smart kids to answer. No one did. So he waited for one of the dumb kids to respond. More silence. Finally, Ben's hand went up. And as it did, his classmates began to whisper and giggle. "Hey, look," someone said. "Carson has his hand up! This oughta be good!"

Mr. Jaeck was surprised too. "Benjamin?"

"That's obsidian," Ben answered. Suddenly, the classroom was quiet. It sounded good. But no one was sure if it was the right answer — or a joke.

"That's right! It *is* obsidian," Mr. Jaeck exclaimed.

No one else was saying anything, so Ben continued: "Obsidian is formed after a volcanic eruption. Lava flows down and when it hits water, there is a super-cooling process. The elements mix together, forcing out the air. Then the surface glazes."

"Right again, Benjamin!" Mr. Jaeck remarked with excitement in his voice. "Class, this is a tremendous piece of information Benjamin has just given us. I'm proud of him." Before he went on with his lesson, Mr. Jaeck asked Ben to stop by after school. His teacher wanted to work on Ben's rock collection with him.

Everyone stared at Ben in astonishment. But the most surprised person in the room was Ben himself. For the first time, he realized that he was not a dummy after all!

Ben also realized that he had known the answer because he'd been reading books. As that sank in, he began to wonder, *What if I read books about all my subjects? Maybe*

I would know more than anyone in the class — more than the kids who tease me and call me names!

Ben had made a giant discovery. But he couldn't yet imagine how much reading would change his life. The truth was he had found the key that would unlock his future and someday enable his greatest dreams to come true.

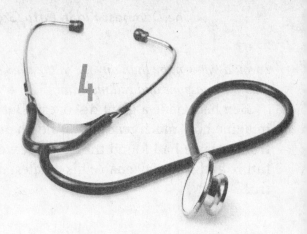

Racial Prejudice and a Spelling Bee

Ben and Curtis encountered racial injustice, but it wasn't as intense as what other black kids faced around the country at that time. Sonya tried to shield her boys from it. For most of their lives, the boys lived in black neighborhoods, attended black schools, and worshiped in black churches.

But one day Ben realized most of his white classmates considered it a disgrace to be black. A student in Ben's fifth-grade class — a white boy named John — had been given the honor of representing the entire school on a television science program broadcast into schools around the state. The entire fifth grade watched eagerly on the day their classmate was scheduled to appear. Ben sat next to a girl named Christine when the two got into a guessing game as to when John's turn would come. So when one segment of the show ended, in an attempt to be the first one to guess, Ben blurted out, "John will be next!"

When a black student walked out on the set instead, some of the kids snickered. Christine leaned over and announced, "I should wring your neck," as if Ben had implied that John was "colored." In that moment, Ben felt a terrible sinking, sick feeling in the pit of his stomach.

Later that same year, Ben experienced another racist incident. One day after school, he was playing with some white children when an angry shout called the white children into the house. Ben began walking away when one of the kids sneaked back out and caught up with him. "We can't play with you anymore 'cause you're a blackie," the child said.

Ben recognized many people thought being black was not a good thing.

The last week of fifth grade, Ben's class held a spelling bee. Just as everyone expected, the winner was Bobby Farmer. But what really surprised Ben was the word that Bobby had to spell in order to win the spelling bee: *agriculture.*

I can spell that word! Ben thought. He had read it just the night before in one of his books. *If I can spell that word, I can learn to spell better than Bobby Farmer.*

That day Ben made up his mind to keep on reading until he was the smartest kid in his class — just like his mother said he could be. He read whenever and wherever he could. He read before school and after school. He read when he was in the bathroom. He read books when he was waiting for the bus.

He kept on reading until, less than two years later, he had gone from the "dumbest kid in fifth grade" to the top of his seventh-grade class at Wilson Junior High School. The same students who had laughed at him on the playground back in the fifth grade now came to him and asked for his assistance with their schoolwork.

Ben liked that. He enjoyed having other students come to him for help. It made him proud to know that he had earned their respect.

* * *

At the junior high school, like at Higgins Elementary, most of the students were white. There too Ben encountered prejudice.

Railroad tracks ran alongside the route that Ben and his brother took to Wilson Junior High. For excitement, they hopped trains on their way to school. Curtis would toss his clarinet onto one flatcar, then jump and catch the railing on the last car of the train. Curtis liked to catch the faster trains. Ben watched for the slower-moving ones. But both boys were placing themselves in great danger. Not only did they have to jump, catch the railing, and hold on, but they also had to watch out for railroad security men who stopped people from hopping the trains.

The security guards never caught Ben or Curtis. But one day when Ben was alone, he got caught by a group of bigger boys, all of them white. One was carrying a very large stick.

The boy hit Ben across his shoulders with the stick,

and the others all crowded around. Ben had nowhere to go. The boys yelled and called Ben ugly racist names.

Ben was small and skinny for his age. He knew he was no match for even one of these boys. No way could he defend himself against all of them, so he just stared at the ground.

"If we ever catch you again, we'll kill you!" one boy yelled before letting Ben go. Ben ran all the way to school and never hopped a train again.

Later that same year, Ben and Curtis tried out for the football team. Neither Carson boy was big, but they were fast. Both did well in practice until one day a group of young, angry white men surrounded them as they were leaving the field. Ben and Curtis were frightened. Finally, one of the white men stepped forward and growled, "You two ever come back, we'll throw you in the river!" That said, the white men turned and walked away.

As the boys hurried home, Ben said to his brother, "Who wants to play football if your own team is against you?"

Curtis agreed. "I think we can find better things to do with our time."

The boys never found out if the young men would have actually hurt them because they never went back to football practice. But it was hard to understand why no one associated with that football team — none of the other players, their parents, or even the coaches — ever asked them why.

Perhaps Ben's worst encounter with racial prejudice

took place during a school assembly. A teacher called Ben to the front of the auditorium to receive the award for the highest academic achievement in his grade. After handing him the award, she turned back to the microphone and tried to shame the white students for letting a black student beat them. "You are not trying hard enough!" she told them. Her message was clear: she thought white kids were smarter than African-American kids and that no black student should have been number one.

Several of Ben's white friends looked at him and rolled their eyes as if to say, "Isn't she ridiculous!"

Ben was angry, but he didn't show it. He wondered what was wrong with her. He had been in her class. She knew how hard he worked and how smart he was. He knew he had earned this award.

By ninth grade, racism no longer came as a shock to Ben, though it still hurt and infuriated him. The last day of his first term in high school, Ben had to carry his report card around from class to class so that each teacher could fill in his grade for that subject. Ben had straight A's in everything going into his last period of the day — physical education. His gym teacher, who was white, looked over all of his grades and then glanced up at Ben. Ben had earned an A in the class, but the teacher wrote in a B — then looked up and grinned. That PE teacher knew he had ruined Ben's chance to make the straight-A honor roll. He also knew there was nothing Ben could do about it.

Ben never told his mother what his PE teacher had

done. He never told her about the kids by the train tracks. Or what the teacher had said at the honors assembly. And neither he nor Curtis ever told her the real reason they quit playing football. They didn't want their mother to worry about them.

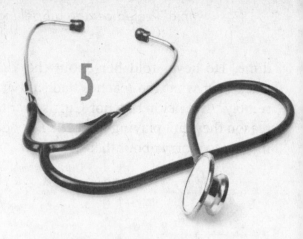

A Change and Not for the Better

Halfway through Ben's eighth-grade year, the Carsons moved back into their old house on Deacon Street. His mother had finally reached the goal she had set years before. The house was small, but it felt like home.

For the entire Carson family, it was a huge dream come true. But it meant Ben changed schools once again. Leaving his friends at Wilson Junior High, he became the "new kid" at Hunter Junior High School.

Ben was still one of the brightest kids in his class. But unlike the students at Wilson, his new classmates didn't seem to care who was smart.

They cared more about who *dressed* smart. And the "in" look was expensive: Italian knit shirts, silk pants, alligator shoes, and stingy-brim hats. Ben's mother had no money for such things.

At Wilson, the other students had respected Ben

because of his intelligence. To be respected at Hunter, you had to dress right, play basketball, and learn how to "cap" people. Capping meant you said something funny—but critical—to get the better of someone.

His first few weeks at Hunter Junior High, Ben served as a favorite target for the other boys to "cap" on. He was new, and his clothing was definitely not "in."

"Know what the Indians did with General Custer's worn-out clothes?" one boy asked.

"Tell us!" another one exclaimed.

"They saved them for our man Carson here!"

"Sure looks it," a third boy chimed in.

"Get close enough and you'll believe it, 'cuz they smell like they're a hundred years old," the first boy said to finish off the "capping."

For several weeks, Ben took this abuse quietly. He didn't know what to do to make friends with his new classmates. *What's wrong with me?* Ben wondered. *Why do I have to be different?*

Then he decided that the best way to survive capping was to become the best capper. Ben thought, *You want to cap? I can show you how to cap!*

The next day, Ben was ready when a ninth grader started it. "Man, that shirt you're wearing has been through World War I, World War II, World War III, and World War IV!"

"Yeah," Ben answered, "and your mama wore it!"

The students standing around all laughed — even the boy who had started the capping. He slapped Ben on the back and said, "Hey, that's okay!"

It didn't take long for the crowd to direct their attention elsewhere. They quickly learned that if they started capping on this new kid, he always had a response to top their remarks.

Ben was thankful for some relief. But he still didn't fit in at his new school. The kids at Hunter seemed to think that if you were poor, you were worthless.

Ben as a grinning teenager.

And Ben knew that his family was still poor even though they were back in their own home. From time to time, Ben's family received food stamps from the government. Without that help, Ben's mother would not have been able to pay the other bills.

But Ben didn't want anyone to know his family used food stamps. So when he went to the grocery store to buy milk or bread, he would carefully watch the checkout area to be sure no one from school was around to see him. If someone he recognized walked in while he was standing in line, he would pretend he'd forgotten something and walk to the back of the store until the coast was clear. Every time he left his house with food stamps in his pocket, he worried that someone would see him use them and they would know that he was poor.

By the start of tenth grade, Ben thought his clothes were his biggest handicap in life. More than anything, he wanted to dress like the "in" group at school. He argued with his mother about it.

"Bennie," his mother said, "what you wear doesn't make any difference."

"But everyone will laugh at me!" Ben responded.

"Only stupid people laugh at someone because of his clothes," his mother answered. "Just because someone dresses better than you doesn't make them better."

Almost every day Ben begged his mother for new clothes. Ben knew he was disappointing his mother with his attitude, but he wanted desperately to be a part of the "in" crowd.

Instead of coming home from school and doing his homework, Ben started staying on the playground, shooting hoops and hanging out with the other guys. Soon his grades slipped from A's to B's, then to C's.

Even though he became one of the gang with his poor grades, the popular crowd still didn't accept him. Ben just wanted to be "cool," so he begged his mother to buy him an Italian knit shirt — if nothing else. Sonya Carson let him know how disappointed she was to hear what he was saying. After all, she thought she'd raised him to be different — not the kind of person who always has to do the same things everyone else is doing. She told him he was too smart to fall for the latest fad and follow people who weren't using their brains.

But Ben told her all he was asking for—all it would take to make him happy—was one Italian knit shirt. That's when his mother made him a deal. "Okay, I'll bring home all the money I make next week and turn it over to you. You'll be in charge of all the family finances. You can buy all the groceries, pay the bills, and take care of all the necessities. Whatever you have left over at the end of the week is yours. You can spend it on Italian knit shirts or whatever else you want."

This is going to be great! Ben thought. He bought the groceries and then began going through the other bills. But he ran out of money long before everything had been paid.

He suddenly realized that his mother, with her third-grade education, had to be some kind of genius just to keep food on the table and any kind of clothes on his back. He'd been complaining and asking her to buy him a $75 shirt when she brought home only $100 a week, working her fingers to the bone scrubbing other people's floors and cleaning other people's toilets.

How could I have been so selfish? he thought.

Ben started studying again, and his grades went back up to A's. Some of his classmates laughed and called him "nerd" and "Poindexter," but he was determined not to let that bother him anymore.

Besides, he could always shut up his teasers and tormentors by saying one thing: "Let's see what I'm doing in twenty years, and then let's see what you're doing in twenty years." Ben not only had a dream, he had a plan for getting there. And the people around him knew it.

Only one major problem stood in the way of reaching his dream.

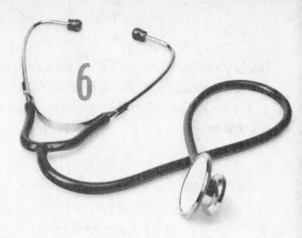

Temper, Temper

From the time he was eight until he was about fourteen, Ben had clung to the dream of becoming a missionary doctor. But he decided he'd lived in poverty long enough. Instead of becoming a missionary doctor, he'd become a psychiatrist instead.

Ben didn't know any psychiatrists, but on television they all looked rich. They lived in fancy mansions, drove Jaguars, and worked in big, plush offices. And all they had to do was talk to crazy people all day long.

Since I seem to be talking to crazy people all day long already, Ben thought, *this is going to work out extremely well.*

Ben started reading *Psychology Today* magazine every month and began making new plans. He'd still be a doctor, just a different kind. There was, however, one major obstacle to Ben's becoming a doctor of any sort.

* * *

One day, during the time Ben wanted expensive clothes, his mother gave him a new pair of pants. Ben looked at them and told her, "I will *not* wear those. They're the wrong kind!"

"What do you mean wrong kind?" his mother asked. She had just gotten home from work and was tired. "You need new pants. Just wear these."

"No!" Ben yelled. And he threw the pants at his mother.

Sonya quietly folded the pants and laid them across the back of a kitchen chair. "I can't take them back. They were on special."

"I don't care! I won't wear them! They're not what I want!"

"Bennie," his mother said, "we don't always get what we want."

"I will!" yelled Ben. He raised his right arm, and his hand flew toward his mother. Curtis, who had been watching, grabbed Ben from behind and wrestled him away from their mother.

Ben was usually a good kid. He seldom got into trouble. But he was definitely having trouble with his temper. He didn't get angry easily, but when he did, he completely lost control. Even now, after almost hitting his mother, Ben didn't want to admit to himself that he had a serious problem with anger.

One day Ben hit a boy in the hallway at school. Because he had the lock from his locker in his hand at the time, the blow opened a three-inch gash in the other student's forehead. Ben ended up in the principal's office. Another time Ben got angry and threw a rock at a kid, breaking the boy's glasses and bloodying his nose.

Each time something like that occurred, Ben brushed it off. *I didn't mean to hurt anyone. I'm a good kid*, he told himself. *I can handle my temper. It's not really a problem.*

Then one day something happened that Ben could no longer ignore. It changed his life forever.

He and his friend Bob were listening to the radio at Bob's house when Bob leaned over and changed to another station. Ben flipped it back. Bob switched stations again. Suddenly Ben lost control. He grabbed the camping knife he carried in his pocket, snapped the blade open, and lunged at Bob's stomach. The blade hit Bob's large metal belt buckle and broke off.

Ben had been so angry, he could have sliced open Bob's belly. Bob could have been lying at Ben's feet bleeding to death. Ben could have been charged with murder and spent the rest of his teen years in juvenile detention. He was very fortunate the knife hit that buckle.

Bob looked at Ben, too shocked to say anything.

Ben muttered, "I ... I ... I'm sorry," then dropped the knife handle and ran home.

There, Ben locked himself in the bathroom and sank to the floor. *I tried to kill my friend!* he thought. *I must be crazy. Only a crazy person would kill a friend.*

He squeezed his eyes shut, but that didn't keep him from seeing, over and over again in his mind, what had just happened: his hand ... the knife ... the broken blade ... Bob's surprised and horrified face. For hours Ben sat there remembering. He felt sick and miserable. Sweat dripped down his back. He was disgusted with himself.

Then he remembered to pray.

In that small bathroom he finally understood that he had a serious problem with his temper. He realized he couldn't control his temper by himself. He needed help. He needed God's help.

Lord, Ben prayed, *you've got to help me. Please take this temper away!*

After a year of reading *Psychology Today* magazine, Ben had learned that a person's temper is a personality trait and that people have to accept their personality traits. Usually you cannot change them. But Ben knew that he would never achieve his dream of being a doctor if he continued to have such problems with his temper.

Lord, he persisted, *please change me. You promise in the Bible that if I ask anything in faith, you will do it. And I believe that you can change me!*

Ben slipped out of the bathroom and got a Bible. Back on the bathroom floor, he opened the Bible to Proverbs. The first verses he saw were about anger and how angry people have nothing but trouble. They seemed to be written just for him. One verse Ben read over and over was Proverbs 16:32, "He who is slow to anger is better than the mighty, and he who rules his spirit than he who takes a city" (RSV).

It was as if God were talking right to Ben. After he had read and prayed for a while, Ben was filled with peace. He stopped crying. His hands quit shaking. He realized God had answered his prayer.

He had been in that bathroom for four hours. But when Ben came out, he knew God had done something in his heart. He had been changed.

Ben had made his decision to trust God, become a Christian, and be baptized back when he was eight years old. But after those four hours in the bathroom when he was fourteen, Ben's faith became personal and heartfelt in a way it had never been before. He began reading the Bible and praying every day.

Ben also realized that he didn't need to be afraid of anything — that the same God who had changed his heart that day in the bathroom was the one who had created the universe. He realized that God was all-powerful and could do anything.

Ben's belief that the Lord wanted him to be a doctor became stronger than ever.

And Ben Carson never again had trouble with his temper.

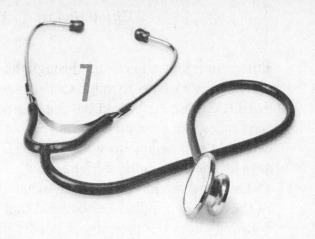

ROTC and College Choices

Ben watched Colonel Sharper striding down the hall of his high school one day during tenth grade. Sharper had a three-diamond cluster on each shoulder, row after row of medals, plus a host of ribbons and even some fancy ropes. It struck Ben that if he joined ROTC — the Reserve Officers' Training Corps — he could wear a snazzy uniform like that to school. Then he would not have to endure the humiliation of wearing outdated clothing.

Colonel Sharper, like Ben's brother, Curtis, was a senior in high school. Curtis had risen to the rank of captain in ROTC and served as the school's company commander. But Sharper was a colonel and one of only three such officers in all the high schools in Detroit.

Students could join ROTC starting the first semester of tenth grade and had six semesters of high school to earn promotions and rise up through the ranks. But Ben was already halfway through tenth grade. If he enrolled in ROTC now, he would be one semester behind his classmates. But even if he was never able to be a colonel, he would still be able to wear an ROTC uniform most days for the remainder of high school. So he signed up.

The clothes may have been what drew him into ROTC, but Ben quickly discovered that he enjoyed everything about the program. He liked military science and strategy, disassembling and assembling rifles, target practice, and drill instruction. By the end of his first semester in ROTC, he was promoted, not to private first class or to corporal, but straight to staff sergeant. Within another few weeks he was promoted to sergeant first class, then master sergeant.

That's when Sergeant Hunt, a real sergeant in the

Ben (third from left) and other members of ROTC.

real Army, challenged Ben to take over the fifth period ROTC class — an unruly band of students who were notoriously disruptive, uncooperative, and exasperating.

Sergeant Hunt promised Ben that if he could shape up the fifth-hour class, he would promote Ben to second lieutenant by the end of his second semester in ROTC. If Ben managed that, he would pass most of the cadets who had started a semester ahead of him. But Ben also knew that he could fail and be humiliated.

Ben did the brave thing. He accepted the sergeant's challenge.

Ben quickly discovered the guys in that fifth-hour class had some pride. So Ben worked them hard on their drilling and their knowledge of rifles. He challenged them to become the top ROTC class in the school by that semester's end. And they did.

Ben received his promotion. He took an ROTC exam and posted the highest score in the city and, after an interview with the ROTC board, was promoted to the rank of lieutenant colonel.

By the end of his junior year of high school, Ben was not only a colonel but also the city executive officer over all the high school ROTC programs in the Detroit public school system. As the ROTC's city executive officer, Ben met General William Westmoreland, had dinner with Congressional Medal of Honor award winners, marched at the head of a Memorial Day parade, and was offered a full scholarship to West Point.

His ROTC experience looked good on Ben's college application, and it bolstered his confidence that he could do well. But he knew that he could not go to West Point and join the military. He didn't want anything to interfere with his longtime dream of becoming a physician.

* * *

While participating in ROTC, Ben also spent the last two years of high school making up for his one year of goofing off. He studied so hard in every subject that by the time he graduated, he had climbed back up to be ranked third academically in his senior class.

That class standing, combined with a high score on the Scholastic Aptitude Test (SAT), meant Ben could go almost anywhere he wanted for college. In addition to the scholarship offer from West Point, the University of Michigan pursued him. But Ben wanted to attend a school farther from home. Representatives came from many colleges to meet with Ben, trying to persuade him to apply to their schools.

By the spring of his senior year of high school, he had narrowed the decision down to two colleges — Harvard or Yale. But Ben didn't know how to decide between them. Clearly, either one could give him a good foundation for medical school. Both were offering him substantial scholarships.

Then one Sunday afternoon Ben was watching one of his favorite television shows, *General Electric College Bowl*, a quiz show where teams from different colleges competed against each other, answering questions about a variety of subjects. The two college teams competing that day were from Harvard and Yale.

Detroit Free Press / William DeKay (5-15-88)

Sonya Carson holds the high school graduation portraits of her sons, Ben, left, and Curtis, right.

Ben was very impressed to see the Yale students blow away Harvard by a score of 510 to 35. Ben's decision was instantly sealed. Forget Harvard. Yale it would be!

During the summers, starting in high school, Ben worked to save money for his college expenses. The summer between his junior and senior years of high school, he worked in a biology laboratory at Wayne State University. The summer after he graduated from high school, Ben wore a shirt and tie to work in the payroll office of the Ford Motor Company.

Whatever job he had, Ben worked as hard as he could.

When he walked onto the Yale campus in the fall of 1969, he expected to impress everyone. After all, he had done great in high school and had scored high on the SAT. Months of listening to college recruiters telling him how much they wanted him to come to their schools had left Ben thinking he was pretty special. *Yale*, he thought, *is lucky I chose to come here.*

He had been on the campus only a week when he began to realize he was not the only bright student at Yale. Ben sat at a table in a dining hall with some fellow freshmen when they began comparing SAT scores. He quickly discovered that everyone at that table had scored higher than he had. That was his first clue that college would be a big step up from high school.

Perhaps that should have scared Ben into working harder at his studies. But it didn't. He had always been able to read and go to classes but not really study until right before a test. Then he would cram for a day or so and make good grades. But that familiar strategy didn't work well for classes at Yale.

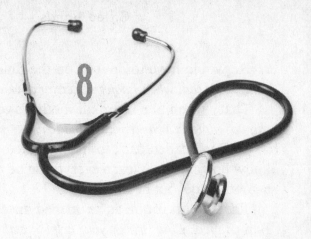

Learning at Yale

Each day, each week of that first semester of college, Ben slipped farther and farther behind in his classes. He fell so far behind that in chemistry, he was not only failing, he had the lowest grade in the class.

The afternoon before his final chemistry exam, Ben walked around the campus, thinking and worrying as the seriousness of his situation sank in. *If I fail chemistry, I won't be able to continue my premed studies. I'll never be a doctor. And that is all I've ever wanted to be!*

He turned the matter over and over in his mind. The only hope he had was a small one. The chemistry professor had a rule. If someone was doing poorly in his class but did very well on the final exam, the professor would toss out the other grades and use just the final exam grade. That was Ben's only chance of passing the course.

He would have to do well on the final. *But how am I going to do that when I don't understand what we've covered?*

That's when Ben heard his mother's voice. *Bennie, you can do whatever you set your mind to do.*

So Ben headed back to his dorm to study. He didn't know how he could learn everything he needed to make a good grade, but he had to try.

There in his room, as he opened his chemistry book, Ben prayed, *Lord, I need your help! I've always thought you wanted me to be a doctor. But I can't be a doctor if I fail this class. Please, either let me know what else I ought to do or perform a miracle and help me pass this exam.*

He studied for hours, reading the textbook, trying to understand what he had not been able to grasp all semester. About midnight, his thoughts began to run together, and the words on the pages blurred.

He flipped off his light and lay down on his bed. Before he drifted off to sleep, he whispered into the darkness, "God, please forgive me for failing you."

During the night, Ben had a strange dream. In his dream, he sat in his chemistry class, the only person there. A shadowy figure walked into the room and began writing chemistry problems on the board. The figure worked the problems and came up with the answers — all while Ben sat and watched.

When Ben woke up the next morning, he clearly remembered what he had seen on the board in the dream. He got up and began writing down the problems. A few of the answers were fuzzy, but he remembered most of the problems with a clarity that surprised him.

Then he showered, dressed, and ate breakfast. As he headed toward his chemistry final, he felt numb from exhaustion and the sure knowledge that he was unprepared for the exam.

He walked into the lecture hall. But unlike his dream, now he was not alone. Ben watched the teacher walk around the room, handing out the test booklets to all six hundred students who would be taking the test that day.

Ben during his first year at Yale.

Ben opened his booklet. The first problem on the page was the same problem that the shadowy figure in his dream had first written on the board. Ben took a deep breath. Was this real? Could this really be happening? He thumbed through the test booklet to confirm what he now suspected. All the problems in the booklet were identical to the ones in his dream.

Ben's pencil flew across the pages. He remembered how to work problem after problem; he knew the answers. Toward the end of the exam, he missed a few where he was beginning to forget the details of the dream. But he knew he would pass!

Ben hurried out of that room and walked around the Yale campus by himself for over an hour. "Thank you, God," he prayed. "You gave me a miracle today!"

Ben also promised that he would never ask God to rescue him like that again. He vowed that he would learn how to study and would work hard throughout each semester, not just at the end. And that is what he did.

From that day on, Ben was more convinced than ever that God wanted him to be a doctor.

* * *

At college, Ben learned another important lesson.

Walking onto the campus of Yale University and into his dormitory, Ben was awed. His modest dorm room offered the nicest living conditions he had known in his entire life. And that was just the beginning. The skinny kid from Detroit's inner city found himself visiting the homes of his professors and fellow students who came from some of the wealthiest families in America.

He could have been envious. Instead, Ben was fascinated by the opportunity to observe the lifestyles of the wealthy. What he saw convinced him that what his mother had always told him and Curtis was true. Rich people were not that much different from everyone else. Great success was possible. But he needed to do more than just wish his circumstances were different. If he wanted to succeed as a doctor, he would have to work hard in his classes and develop skills that would be valuable in the world around him.

At the same time, Ben noted that wealth could also be a handicap. Many of his fellow students did not seem to appreciate the value of a dollar the way he had been taught to do. They spent money on sophisticated stereo equipment for their dorm rooms, expensive outings to New York City, and lavish dates. Money created a distraction for many students that kept them from focusing on their studies. Some flunked out of school their first year.

Seeing this, Ben realized that in one sense, his lack of money, which made him feel self-conscious at first, actually contributed to his academic success. Without the opportunities and distractions money could buy, he found it easier to keep up with his studies.

* * *

Ben still needed to have a job in the summers to make some money. The summer following his first year at Yale, Ben found work in highway trash collection. He supervised a crew of six guys whose job was to walk along interstate highways picking up litter. The highway department had several such crews, and most of their workers picked up an average of two bags of trash each day.

Ben knew his guys could do that much in an hour if they worked harder. So he struck a deal with his crew. If they would come to work at six in the morning, hours ahead of the other litter crews, and collect a total of 150 bags of trash — 25 bags each — they could then go home. And they would be paid for the whole day.

Ben's workers agreed to the deal and made a contest of it, competing with each other to see who could collect the most trash in the shortest amount of time. They worked in the cool of the morning and often got back to the Department of Transportation in time to see the other crews just starting to work. They laughed and teased the other crews who were headed out in the heat of the day with long hours of work ahead of them.

Ben knew he wasn't following the instructions he'd been given for his crew. But since his guys kept setting records for the most trash collected, no one ever complained.

What Ben did not understand then was how finding such creative approaches to work would help him as a doctor. Indeed, one of the characteristics that would one day make him a great doctor was his ability to see new and better ways to get things done.

* * *

Even though he found good jobs and worked hard every summer, Ben had little money to spend during the school year. Once during his sophomore year, when he was broke, he walked across campus, thinking and praying, *Lord, please help me. I need at least enough money for bus fare to get to church.*

As Ben approached the old college chapel, he looked down and saw a ten-dollar bill lying on the ground. *Thank you, Lord!*

During his junior year, he hit the same low point — not enough money for bus fare or a phone call. He took another walk across campus to the chapel, looking on the ground for money the entire way, but found nothing.

That same day he had to retake a test. According to a posted notice, the exam papers from a psychology test he had taken a few days earlier had been "inadvertently burned." So Ben headed over to class to take the test again.

The professor handed out the exams to the 150 students and then left. Ben began reading the questions. *Whoa! These are much, much more difficult than the questions on the original test!*

Evidently, Ben wasn't the only person who thought so. After a moment, another student spoke up: "Can you believe this? I can't answer these! They're too hard! I'm leaving. I'll tell the professor that I didn't see the notice about the retest. They'll have to offer the test again, and I'll know what to study the next time." With that, the student got up and left the classroom. Soon other students decided to do the same thing.

Ben kept staring at the test. It wasn't fair! *But I have to try and do my best*, he thought. *I won't lie and say I didn't see the notice.*

Ben kept working, occasionally hearing other students get up and walk out. Half an hour later, he was the only student left in the room.

Suddenly, the door swung open and the professor walked in. With her was a photographer who walked over and took Ben's picture.

"What's going on?" Ben asked.

"A hoax," the professor replied. "We wanted to see who the most honest person in this class is. And you won!" Then the professor handed Ben his reward: a ten-dollar bill.

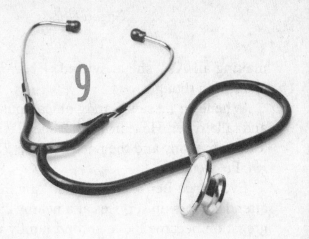

Ben and Candy

Ben worked so hard to pay his bills and make the best grades in college that he found little time for dating or even thinking about girls. When he met Candy Rustin just before his third year at Yale, he almost missed out on love.

Each year, Yale hosted a reception for incoming freshmen from Michigan at the Grosse Pointe Country Club. Upperclassmen from Michigan were on hand to welcome the new students. At the reception, Ben noticed a pretty young woman with a bubbly laugh who seemed to be talking to everyone. *That is one good-looking girl!* he thought.

Sometime after the semester started, Ben spotted Candy again, walking across campus. He smiled and asked how she was doing in her classes. "I think I'm making all A's," she answered. *Wow! She must be really smart*, Ben thought.

Whenever he saw Candy on campus, he would stop and talk to her. He learned that she played violin for the Yale Symphony and the Bach Society. *This is one talented girl*, he decided.

Ever since Ben's first year at Yale, he had regularly attended worship services at a nearby church. The congregation became like a second family for him. Nearly every week after services, a family would invite Ben and his roommate to eat dinner with them. Ben sang in the choir, and Aubrey Tompkins, the choir director, often gave Ben a ride to and from church.

With Ben's encouragement, Candy auditioned to be the organist for that choir. She didn't get the job, but she stayed to sing in the choir. Now she and Ben saw each other around campus during the week and at church on weekends. Before long, they both began attending a church-sponsored Bible study and meeting after classes to talk. But they were still just friends — both too busy with school to think about being anything more.

During the Thanksgiving holiday the following year, Ben and Candy were hired by the university to interview students from Michigan who had high SAT scores. Ben rented a car and the two drove from town to town, meeting with students in the Detroit area who wanted to attend Yale. Between appointments, they spent time visiting their own friends and families.

On the last day of their holiday, Ben and Candy were late getting started on the drive back to Yale. Ben had to return the rental car by eight the next morning in New Haven. To make that deadline, they needed to drive all night.

But Ben was already exhausted. "I don't know if I can stay awake," he told Candy as they headed back to Connecticut. Shortly after they crossed the state line into Ohio, Candy fell asleep. Ben let her doze, knowing that their recruiting trip had left her tired too.

Cruising along at about one in the morning, Ben noticed a sign, "Youngstown, Ohio." They were making such good progress, Ben felt confident they would make it back on time after all.

The car was comfortably warm. Candy slept peacefully in the passenger seat. Few vehicles shared the road at that time of morning. In fact, it had been several minutes since Ben had even seen another car when he drifted off to sleep at the wheel.

The vibration of the tires as they hit the metal illuminators separating the lanes woke Ben. All he saw ahead was the blackness of a deep ravine at the side of the road, and the car was heading straight toward it.

Ben took his foot off the accelerator and jerked the wheel as hard as he could to turn back onto the roadway. The car could have flipped. But instead it went into a spin — turning 'round and 'round on the highway.

Ben took his hands off the steering wheel as scenes of his childhood flashed through his mind. *This must be what it's like to die*, he thought.

When the car finally stopped spinning, it was in the far right lane of the highway — the motor still running, pointing in the right direction. Shaking, Ben eased the car off onto the shoulder of the road. A split second later, a large eighteen-wheeler barreled past.

Ben shut the motor off and sat in the darkness. "We're alive. God saved our lives! Thank you, God," he said out loud. Ben's voice woke Candy, who had slept through the whole incident.

"Is something wrong, Ben?" she asked. "Why are we stopped?"

"We're all right," Ben assured her.

But Candy persisted, "Then why did we stop? What's going on?"

Ben started the car and began to pull back onto the road.

"Ben, please tell me," Candy begged.

Ben pulled off the road, took a deep breath, and admitted, "I fell asleep back there, and ... I thought we were both going to die."

Candy reached over and took Ben's hand. "The Lord spared us. He must have a plan for us." After that neither Ben nor Candy could go back to sleep. They talked and drove until sunrise.

At one point, Candy asked Ben, "Why are you so nice to me?"

"I guess I'm just a nice guy," he said.

"Ben, be serious!" she insisted.

"Because I like you," he confessed.

"I like you a lot too," Candy told him, "more than anyone else."

Ben eased the car back off the road and pulled to a

Ben's graduation from Yale with Sonya and Candy.

stop. He turned to Candy and kissed her — their first kiss. From then on, Ben and Candy were inseparable. They did their homework together. They encouraged each other. They were in love.

* * *

During his final year of college, Ben applied to medical schools. Unlike many of his classmates who were worried about which medical school would accept them, Ben was confident that he would go to the University of Michigan School of Medicine. He believed so firmly that God wanted him to be a doctor that he never doubted he would be accepted.

One day another student who was agonizing about his own medical school applications turned to Ben and asked, "Carson, aren't you worried?"

"No," Ben answered. "I'm going to the University of Michigan."

"How can you be sure?" the friend demanded to know.

"Easy," Ben replied. "My Father owns the university."

Ben never did explain that the Father he was talking about was his heavenly Father, the one who created the universe and, therefore, owns everything in it, including all the universities. And Ben was right. The University of Michigan School of Medicine accepted him almost immediately.

Candy still had two more years at Yale, which meant they would be apart for most of that time. But they vowed to write to each other every single day.

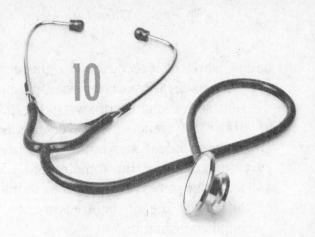

Medical School Struggles

That summer between college and medical school, Ben needed a job. But he couldn't find work anywhere around Detroit. Companies were laying off people, not hiring. Since his mother was caring for the children of the president of Sennett Steel, Sonya spoke to Mr. Sennett about her son's problem. He told her to send Ben to his company.

His first day at Sennett Steel, some men showed Ben how to operate an overhead boom crane. They let him practice for a while, then tested him on the machine. At the end of the day, they said, "You can handle this crane."

For them to give that responsibility to a young man just out of college was amazing. Ben had to drive the crane and maneuver tons of steel through narrow passageways, then carefully load the steel onto trucks. He had to work the levers exactly right to swing the boom over tall stacks of material, then pick up and balance the steel so it didn't tip or swing. He had to know how to "brake" the crane with a reverse action on the trolley and come to a dead stop at the wall instead of swinging past it and crashing into something. He also had to load and stack the pieces of steel so they didn't damage or fall off the trucks. The job required an enormous amount of eye-hand coordination.

In the course of that summer, Ben discovered that he had an unusual ability — a gift from God — to think and see in three dimensions. He could visualize just how the steel needed to move and where it would fit. These special abilities, which enabled him to maneuver and precisely place huge pieces of steel with that boom crane, would one day help him see his surgical patients in three dimensions.

When the summer was over, Ben headed to medical school at the University of Michigan. Being separated from Candy wasn't the only difficult part of his medical school experience. His classes were much harder than he had imagined.

Despite Ben's success at Yale, he struggled as a first-year med student. Just six weeks into the semester, Ben did so poorly on a big exam that he had to talk to his adviser.

"Mr. Carson," the adviser said, "you seem like an intelligent young man. There are many things you could do besides being a doctor."

Ben was devastated! He'd dreamed of being a doctor

since he was eight years old. Now his adviser thought Ben wasn't smart enough to handle medical school. He recommended that Ben drop out.

When Ben refused, the adviser suggested Ben take half as many classes. That meant Ben's medical school would take twice as long, and he didn't want to do that.

Ben still believed God wanted him to be a doctor. So he decided to think about why he was struggling and come up with a strategy for solving the problem.

Ben soon realized it was not whether he could learn — but how. His classes were all lectures, which meant six to eight hours every day sitting in a classroom listening. Nothing seemed to be sinking in. He knew he had never learned well from lectures. Ben had always learned best by reading. He needed to find a way to use that strength.

For the rest of his time at the University of Michigan, Ben skipped most of his class lectures. Instead, he spent hours reading in his room or at the library. He read textbooks. He studied all sorts of related resources. He paid other students to take notes in his classes, and he read and studied those notes. He even made flash cards for each of his classes and used those to study. Plus, he attended all the labs for the hands-on experiments.

Ben's new study strategy worked. His schoolwork was much better; he not only shocked his adviser, he surprised himself.

Medical school was never easy for Ben. He studied so long and had so much material to cover that he often fell asleep reading his assignments. To keep himself awake, Ben walked around his dorm room as he read. He also learned to pace himself by reading for forty-five minutes, then rewarding himself with fifteen minutes to do anything he wished.

* * *

Ben's ability to see in three dimensions, which had helped him work the crane at Sennett Steel, enabled Ben to come up with a new surgical technique while still a student in medical school. One day, Ben watched a professor— a neurosurgeon — during surgery. "The hardest part is finding the foramen ovale," the surgeon told his students as they watched him probe the back of the patient's head with a long needle. (The foramen ovale is a little hole at the base of the skull.)

There ought to be an easier way, Ben thought. *Surely there's another approach that works better.*

After class he went to the radiology lab where he had worked one summer. His friends there let him use the equipment, and Ben began to experiment. It took him several days, but Ben hit upon an idea to use two small metal rings and an X-ray to locate the foramen ovale on patients without having to poke them again and again with a needle.

At first he didn't want to tell the doctors about his discovery. After all, he was just a medical student. They were professors and neurosurgeons with years of experience. *If I'm wrong*, Ben thought, *I'll embarrass myself. If I'm right, these surgeons might be offended that a medical student came up with a new procedure.* But after Ben had a few chances to try his technique, he was convinced it really worked. He finally showed his teachers what he had discovered, and a senior professor said, "That's fabulous, Carson." Soon all the doctors were using Ben's new technique.

* * *

By the last year of medical school, Ben had important decisions to make: where to do his internship and residency, and what area of medicine he wanted to specialize in.

As he considered a specialty, Ben thought, *What is it that I'm really good at? I have excellent hand-eye coordination. I'm a very careful person. And I am fascinated by the human brain. I loved doing my two rotations in neurosurgery ... I believe I would make a great brain surgeon!*

There was no way Ben could imagine where that decision would take him.

The two brothers at Ben's graduation from medical school.

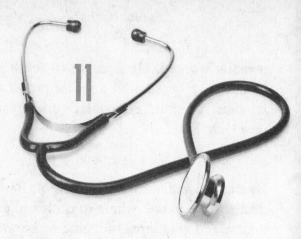

Maranda Francisco

When Candy graduated from Yale and Ben was between his second and third years of medical school, one of the happiest and most exciting days of Ben's life arrived: the day he and Candy were married.

For the first years of marriage, Ben and Candy lived in a small apartment in Ann Arbor, Michigan, while Ben finished his work at the University of Michigan.

When Ben decided he wanted to specialize in neurosurgery, he applied for an internship and residency at Johns Hopkins Medical Institutions — perhaps the best and most famous training hospital in the world. Once he was accepted, the young couple moved to Baltimore, Maryland.

On his first day at Johns Hopkins, Ben walked toward a nurses' station wearing green scrubs. A nurse looked up

Ben and Candy's wedding in Ann Arbor, Michigan, on July 6, 1975.

at him and asked, "Who did you come to pick up?" She thought he was an orderly.

"I'm not here to pick up anyone." Ben smiled. "I'm the new intern."

The nurse stammered an apology.

"That's okay," Ben said, "I'm new. Why should you know who I am?"

Ben did his residency at Johns Hopkins from 1978 until 1982. During that time, Ben encountered other people who were surprised to see an African-American doctor on the staff at the famous hospital. Once in a while a patient would tell Ben's supervisor, Dr. Long, they didn't want to be treated by a black physician. Each time Dr. Long told them, "You're free to leave whenever you wish. But if you stay, Dr. Carson will be your doctor." No one ever walked out.

For a time, Candy worked for an insurance company, then got a job at the hospital as an assistant to one of the chemistry professors. Ben put in such long hours as a resident, he was seldom home. So Candy used her time to go back to school. She earned a master's degree in business administration and landed a banking job.

During his residency, Ben mastered the basics of neurosurgery. He also conducted research studies and impressed his teachers with both his surgical skills and his character. By the time he completed his training, the head of his department invited him to stay and serve on the faculty. But Ben and Candy had another adventure in mind.

Ben had met an Australian neurosurgeon who kept telling him, "You should come to my country and be a senior registrar (a job similar to being a chief resident in the United States) at our teaching hospital in Perth."

At first, Ben didn't take the offer seriously. But his Australian friend kept talking, and Ben kept listening. Finally, he and Candy sensed that God was leading them to Australia. They spent every bit of their savings for two one-way airline tickets and took off for the other side of the world.

The teaching hospital where Ben worked was a major center for neurosurgery for the entire continent. During his year in Australia, Ben gained more experience in performing various techniques than some surgeons receive throughout a lifetime practicing in the United States.

Johns Hopkins Medical Institution.

When his year in Australia was over, Ben and Candy returned to the States. They brought with them their newborn son, Murray.

Ben was welcomed back to a spot on the faculty at Johns Hopkins. A few months after that, Ben was asked to be the chief of pediatric neurosurgery. He was only thirty-three years old.

Less than a year later, about the time the Carsons' second son, BJ (short for Ben Jr.), was born, Ben met a young patient named Maranda Francisco. Other doctors had given this four-year-old girl and her parents no hope of recovery. But Ben decided to try a different approach to Maranda's problem.

When Ben first saw Maranda, she was having as many as a hundred seizures each day. Ben noted that the seizures always began with trembling at the right corner of Maranda's mouth. Then the right side of her face would twitch. Then her right arm and right leg would begin to jerk until the whole right side of her body was moving. Finally, she would go limp.

By the time Maranda arrived at the hospital, she had almost stopped eating out of fear that she might choke. She was also forgetting how to walk and talk, needed constant supervision, and required lots of medication.

For several weeks, Ben studied Maranda's records. After noting that all the seizures began on her right side, Ben determined that the cause lay somewhere in the left side of her brain. He discussed the case with one of his colleagues, and they began to consider a drastic idea.

Ben read all the articles and papers he could find about a procedure called a "hemispherectomy," a surgery in which one entire side — half — of a patient's brain is removed. The procedure had been attempted decades earlier with little or no success. But technology and surgical techniques had improved greatly since then. *Maybe*, Ben thought, *just maybe the surgery could now be done successfully.*

Ben knew that Maranda's surgery would be one of the most difficult he had ever attempted. He also knew the outcome could change his career and the attitudes of other doctors toward a controversial procedure. There were many unanswered questions.

The left half of the brain controls speech. If Ben

removed it, would Maranda still be able to talk? With half of her brain gone, would she be able to see or walk? Because the left side of the brain controls the right side of the body, would the surgery leave Maranda paralyzed on the right side? No one knew the answers to any of these questions.

What Ben did know was this: the disease that had damaged this little girl's brain was getting worse. Unless the seizures could be stopped, Maranda would die.

Finally Ben spoke with Maranda's parents. "I'm willing to do a hemispherectomy. But I have never done one before. Maranda might die on the operating table. Or we might damage the other side of her brain."

"What will happen if we don't do the surgery?" her parents asked.

"She will get worse and then die," Ben answered.

"If there is any chance," her parents said, "we want you to operate."

The evening before the surgery, Ben visited Maranda and her parents in her hospital room. He went over all the information about the procedure with them one more time. Then he told them, "I have a homework assignment for you. I give this to every patient and their family before surgery."

"Whatever you want us to do," Maranda's father said, puzzled that this doctor thought there was something he and his wife could do.

"Say your prayers tonight," Ben said. "I believe prayer helps."

Maranda's parents agreed.

Ben promised that he too would pray. And that night, before Ben went to bed, he asked God to guide his hands and give life back to Maranda Francisco.

The next day in the operating room, from the beginning, things did not go well. Maranda's brain had been so damaged by her seizures that wherever the doctors touched it, the tissue began to bleed. Wherever Ben cut, small blood vessels had to be sealed carefully and blood had to be suctioned away before he could see what to do next.

Ben's surgical team included another surgeon, Dr. Neville Knuckey, as well as nurses, technicians, and anesthesiologists. The excessive bleeding kept them all busy. Slowly, meticulously, for more than eight hours, Ben separated the left side of Maranda's brain from the right side. As he worked, Ben kept asking God to guide his hands.

Almost ten hours after she was taken into surgery, Maranda's skull was stitched back into place and the doctors stepped away from the table. They had successfully removed the left side of the little girl's brain. But no one knew what that might mean. Would Maranda's seizures stop? Would she be able to speak?

Ben followed the gurney carrying Maranda out of the operating room. Maranda's parents heard them coming down the hall. Running from the waiting room to see their daughter, Mrs. Francisco leaned over and kissed her little girl. Maranda's eyes opened slightly, and in a small voice she said, "I love you, Mommy and Daddy." The question about whether Maranda would be able to speak had been answered. Then Maranda squirmed around a little on the gurney, moving her right arm and right leg, proving that her right side was not paralyzed.

News that Maranda had survived the surgery and that she had spoken moved quickly through the hospital. Best of all, the seizures did not return!

Maranda's surgery was the first of numerous hemispherectomies Ben

Maranda Francisco at the hospital party after her successful surgery.

Carson would perform. Most of the children he treats are referred to Johns Hopkins by other doctors who feel they don't have enough experience to treat the conditions. For that reason, Ben sees many patients with complicated problems who are extremely ill. He's become an expert in surgical treatment for all sorts of seizures — whether they are caused by brain tumors, accidents, birth defects, or developmental problems. Many of these patients, like Maranda, come to Johns Hopkins as a last resort. Many have been cured of their seizures, recovered, and gone on to live normal lives.

Two of Ben's most famous patients, born in Germany in February 1987 (just two months after the birth of Ben and Candy's third son, Rhoeyce), were twin brothers — Patrick and Benjamin Binder. Their arrival at Johns Hopkins would change Ben's life every bit as much as he changed theirs.

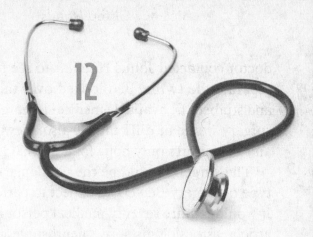

Patrick and Benjamin Binder

Patrick and Benjamin were craniopagus Siamese twins. That means when the boys were born, their heads were attached. Twins like this are so rare that it happens only once in every two million births. And most craniopagus Siamese twins die at birth.

Doctors do not understand what causes this to happen. Most believe the twins grow from one egg that doesn't completely separate. A few believe the babies separate, then grow back together.

Patrick and Benjamin seemed to be healthy babies in every other way. Their heads were joined at the back, so they were facing away from each other. That meant they couldn't move like normal babies. As long as they remained attached, they would never be able to walk, crawl, sit, or turn over. They couldn't even see each other.

Not long after their birth, the Binder babies' German

doctor contacted Johns Hopkins to see if surgery could separate the twins. Ben looked over the boys' records and studied the available medical research. He knew the surgery would be difficult. He also knew it was Patrick's and Benjamin's only hope for a normal life.

The surgery would be the challenge of a lifetime, a type of surgery Ben could expect to perform only once. It would require seventy medical personnel: seven pediatric anesthesiologists, five neurosurgeons, two cardiac surgeons, five plastic surgeons, and dozens of nurses and technicians all working together in one operating room.

Ben and three other doctors who would be involved, Craig Dufresne, Mark Rogers, and David Nichols, planned to fly to Europe to examine the boys and meet their parents. While there, Dr. Dufresne would insert balloons under the twins' scalps to help stretch the skin. The extra skin would be needed to cover the boys' skulls after they were separated. Growing so much new skin would take several months.

But just two weeks before Ben was scheduled to fly to Germany, burglars broke into the Carsons' home. Among the items stolen was Ben's passport. He couldn't go overseas without it.

Ben asked the police investigating the break-in if they thought he might get his papers back. "No chance," the police responded. "The thieves will just throw them away."

Ben called the passport office. "I'm sorry, Dr. Carson," he was told. "We can't replace your passport in such a short time."

"Lord," Ben prayed, "if you want me to help with this surgery, you'll have to get me a passport."

Two days later, the police called. A detective had found Ben's passport and other stolen documents in a garbage container. Ben was able to go to Germany to examine the twins after all.

The surgical team at Johns Hopkins spent five months preparing for the separation surgery. They had five three-hour dress rehearsals, during which they practiced the procedure with life-size dolls attached with Velcro. After each practice round, the medical personnel would discuss the procedure in detail, trying to anticipate anything that could go wrong and how it should be handled. They even marked where each person would stand in the overcrowded operating room.

The doctors' plan was to use a combination of hypothermia, circulatory bypass, and deliberate cardiac arrest. The babies' temperatures would be lowered in order to slow their bodily functions. A bypass would circulate each boy's blood through a heart-lung machine. Doctors also decided to intentionally stop the boys' hearts from beating. All three techniques had never been used at the same time. But the surgeons believed the combined strategy offered the best hope to prevent brain damage.

Finally, on September 5, 1987, at 7:15 in the morning, the doctors began the surgery to separate the seven-month-old twins.

The anesthesiologists gave the babies medicine to help them sleep through the surgery. The heart surgeons

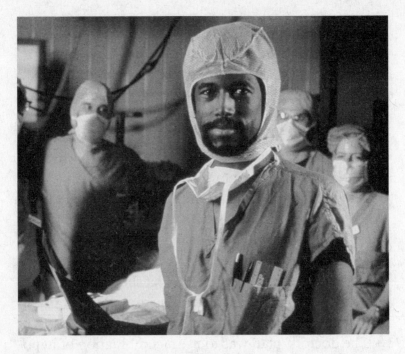

Dr. Carson in scrubs, preparing for surgery.

inserted monitors to keep track of how well the boys' hearts were doing.

Next, Ben began the incisions in the babies' scalp. He cut away an area of the skull, preserving the bone so it could be used to shape and build two separate skulls for the boys.

The doctors then worked on the dura, the tough membrane that covers the brain. This had many irregularities that Ben and the other doctors had to work around. Slowly and carefully they snipped and cut at the places where the two boys were joined.

When the doctors came to the part of the boys' brains called the torcula, they found the twins shared a single torcula that was much larger than normal. Ben started to cut the torcula to divide it, and the babies began to bleed profusely.

The doctors immediately connected the twins to heart-lung machines that chilled their blood from 95 degrees to 68 degrees Fahrenheit. They also stopped the hearts of both boys and turned off the heart-lung machines, halting the blood flow in the babies' bodies. The boys were now in hypothermic arrest. This allowed the doctors to separate the brains of both boys and rebuild the twins' blood vessels without the boys bleeding to death.

But they could leave the babies in hypothermic arrest for only one hour. After that, if the machines were not turned back on to circulate warmed blood back through the boys' bodies, brain damage would occur.

Everyone in the room understood the surgery was now a life-or-death race against the clock. The entire team worked together, all members doing their part. Twenty minutes later, Ben cut the final blood vessel that connected the two boys. For the first time in their lives, Patrick and Benjamin Binder were two separate individuals.

Ben took over the surgery on one baby, and Dr. Donlin Long took over on the other. They had forty minutes left to rebuild the blood vessels for each child so blood could flow through them. Doctors had thought this part of the surgery would take almost an hour — too long.

To save time, the heart surgeons looked over the shoulders of Dr. Carson and Dr. Long to see what sizes and shapes of replacement tissue would be needed to reconstruct the blood vessels. They cut pieces of pericardium (tissue from around the heart) to match. The doctors did such a good job that Ben and Dr. Long were able to work much faster. Dr. Long finished his twin first. Ben finished his baby with only seconds to spare.

"It's done!" someone said. The heart-lung machines were turned back on and the babies' blood began to flow again. But the danger wasn't over.

For the next three hours, the doctors fought to control the bleeding from small blood vessels that had been cut during the surgery. Because the blood had had to be thinned to run through the heart-lung machine, it would no longer clot. Every blood vessel that could bleed did bleed. The surgical team tied off or joined the ends of the tiny blood vessels as fast as they could. To replace the blood the boys were losing, doctors kept giving the babies more and more blood.

Until there was no more — the hospital blood bank was out. Calls were made all over Baltimore; the proper blood type was finally located at the Red Cross Blood Bank. They had ten pints, which turned out to be exactly what the surgeons needed to finish the surgery.

But even after the doctors got the bleeding under control, there was no time to celebrate. The twins' brains were beginning to swell so fast Ben was afraid the surgeons wouldn't be able to get the scalps closed. So they gave the boys a drug to put them into a coma and slow down their brain activity.

Finally, Ben and the other neurosurgeon stepped

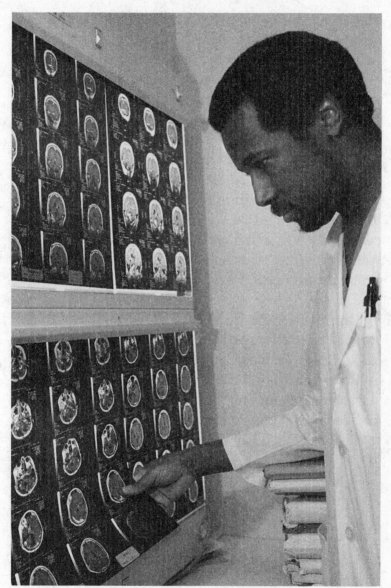

Dr. Carson looks at a patient's brain scans.

back to let the plastic surgeons piece the skulls back together and cover the bone with the scalp tissue. Twenty-two hours after the surgery began, the team walked out of the operating room. One of the staff doctors went to the twins' mother and, with a smile on his face, asked, "Which child would you like to see first?"

Ben knew the surgery was just the first step — though a giant step — in the twins' long road to recovery. He began to pray, *Oh, God, let both boys live. Let them make it!*

Patrick and Benjamin Binder remained in a coma for ten days. During that time, their parents and doctors could only wait and hope ... and pray. Would the boys wake up? Would they be able to live normal lives? Ben kept telling himself, *It's all in God's hands. That's where it's always been.*

One day in the middle of the second week, Ben stopped by to check on the twins. "They're moving!" he said. "Look! He moved his left foot. See?"

Later that day, both boys opened their eyes and started looking around. "He can see! They both can see! He's looking at me!" someone exclaimed.

"Thank you! Thank you!" Ben told God again and again.

A few months later, Theresa and Franz Binder went home to Germany with their beloved twin boys. By then, the publicity surrounding the case had made Ben a celebrity. He began to receive referrals from doctors around the country and around the world. He suddenly was in great demand as a speaker, telling his story to all kinds of audiences — young and old.

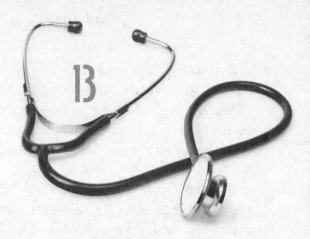

The Makwaeba Twins – Why?

Ben thought the Binder surgery was a once-in-a-lifetime case. But he was wrong. Seven years after that surgery, Ben was given a second opportunity to operate on craniopagus Siamese twins.

In January 1994, Ben received a phone call at work. A man said, "My name is Dr. Samuel Mokgokong. I am professor of neurosurgery at the Medical University of South Africa at Medunsa."

"How may I help you?" Ben asked.

Dr. Mokgokong explained that he was caring for a set of South African Siamese twins whose case seemed similar to that of the Binder twins. He was hoping Ben would be willing to help in the separation of the two little girls who were his patients.

Less than a month later, Dr. Mokgokong came to the United States and brought all the necessary records for

Ben to review. The twins were named Nthabiseng and Mahlatse Makwaeba, and though they were smaller than the Binders had been, they seemed to have about the same degree of attachment at the back of their heads. Ben believed there was a fair chance both girls could be saved.

But when Dr. Mokgokong asked if Ben could go to Medunsa to lead the surgical team, Ben knew the circumstances would be different. The surgery on the Binder twins had taken months of careful planning. The surgical team had been made up of the finest medical personnel Johns Hopkins had to offer, doctors Ben was used to working with. In Medunsa, he would be operating with doctors he hardly knew.

There was another problem. Johns Hopkins Hospital is one of the best medical facilities in the United States. Would a hospital in Medunsa, South Africa, have all that would be needed to pull off such a procedure? Did they even have the necessary equipment? Such a surgery had never before been attempted on the continent of Africa.

As Ben prayed about his decision, he remembered the Binder twins. Their surgery had catapulted him to surprising prominence as a surgeon. It had opened doors throughout the world medical community. It had led to opportunities Ben had never dreamed possible. He had been invited to speak to audiences he would not have been able to reach before.

When he thought about all the things that had happened because of the Binder twins' surgery, he wondered,

Does God want to use another pair of Siamese twins to change a country like South Africa?

Ben could hardly wait to see what would happen on his trip to Medunsa. He sent Dr. Mokgokong home with a list of equipment they would need for the operation along with suggestions for the sixty doctors, nurses, and technicians they would need.

When Ben arrived in South Africa, Dr. Mokgokong met his flight with bad news. The twins were sick — too sick, he believed, to undergo the surgery. When Ben examined the Makwaeba sisters, he agreed. The girls would need a couple of months to regain their strength.

But Ben's visit gave him a chance to meet the surgical team and discuss strategies with them face-to-face. Ben also got a firsthand look at the facilities in Medunsa. They were very different from those in American hospitals.

The patients were cared for in large open-air wards with twenty to thirty beds each. The windows were open, and breezes carried in whatever was in the air outside — dust, leaves, pollen, and, occasionally, bugs.

Ben walked around inside the hospital and saw doctors and nurses caring for their patients. He was impressed with the good health care they were providing.

Ben returned home sooner than he had planned but with a greater sense of confidence. The procedure was rescheduled for June.

While Ben waited to return to South Africa, he received another honor. Each year, *Essence* magazine gave the Essence Award to African-American women they judged to have made a significant and notable contribution to the world. In 1994, for the first time, African-American men would receive the prestigious Essence Award. Ben was one of the men chosen.

Ben and Candy flew to New York City for the presentation ceremony. He looked around at the well-known crowd and saw the Reverend Jesse Jackson, movie director Spike Lee, actor Denzel Washington, and comedian Eddie Murphy. They all were being honored. Ben realized that had he not been involved in the separation of the Binder twins back in 1987, he would not be sitting there.

June came, and Ben traveled back to South Africa. He faced a difficult decision: the Makwaeba twins were even sicker than they had been in April. The girls' hearts were getting so weak that surgery seemed to be their only hope. If they weren't separated soon, they would die.

The doctors gathered the whole medical team together and informed them of the intention to proceed. Everyone knew the girls were not doing well. To make things even more stressful, an American network television camera crew had arrived to record the whole procedure.

Like the surgery on the Binder twins, this operation required several neurosurgeons plus heart surgeons, plastic surgeons, and a host of nurses and technicians. The operating rooms had brand-new ventilators, new surgical tools, and state-of-the-art monitors for the anesthesiologists and cardiovascular surgeons.

Two surgical tables were set up so they could be pulled apart at the moment of separation. Then two different teams would quickly surround each twin to close their skulls and scalps. Remembering the rather frightening situation that had occurred during the operation on the Binder twins, Ben instructed the hospital to stockpile a large supply of blood.

The operation began with the plastic surgeons carefully removing the scalp expanders they had put in place months earlier. When they finished, the neurosurgical team went to work.

When Ben cut through the skull, the bone proved to be unusually bloody. So he spent a lot of time trying to control the blood loss. After the fused sections of skull had been cut away, Ben could see that the underlying dura (the thick leather-like membrane that surrounds the brain) was connected between the twins in a complex way. It had to be carefully cut and separated.

The doctors found large pools of blood called "venous lakes" and a great number of blood vessels connecting the two brains. More than a dozen hours into the surgery, it became obvious that the doctors needed to hook up each of the twins to a heart-lung bypass machine that would slowly drain and cool their blood. This would bring the babies' bodily functions to a near halt. The hearts would stop pumping, and the blood would stop flowing. As before, the team had only one hour after the hearts were stopped to complete their work before brain damage would occur.

Within that hour, the doctors had to separate all the

interwoven blood vessels. The doctors quickly sorted out all the connections and carefully divided the shared vessels before time ran out. They began pumping blood back to the babies, but the smaller twin died. Her tiny heart would not begin beating. By then, the surgery had lasted fifteen hours.

Now all the doctors, as a team, concentrated on the other girl. A few hours later, when they completed the operation, she seemed to be in pretty good condition. She even moved a little in the recovery room. Although sad about the death of one child, everyone was glad the second twin had been saved.

But a few hours after surgery, the second girl began having seizures, and her condition steadily worsened. She died two days later.

When doctors examined her body, they found her kidneys had stopped working. They learned the girls had been entirely symbiotic — they depended completely on each other for life. The smaller child had relied on the larger girl's heart, and the larger girl needed her smaller sister's kidneys. But even if they had remained together, the heart and the kidneys would have soon failed. The girls would have died anyway.

But that knowledge wasn't much comfort for the family or the doctors.

On the morning before he left for home, Ben was interviewed on a news show, *Good Morning, South Africa*. He tried to explain what had happened, to let people know that no hospital in the world would have been able to save the two little girls. But he felt discouraged. He had hoped and prayed for these children. He had believed that God would work a miracle. Yet the girls had died.

As the plane lifted off the ground in South Africa, taking him back home, Ben prayed, *God, why did you get me involved in a situation like this where there was never any possibility for success? Why did you let me spend so much valuable time and energy in something that could not possibly work out? Why would you provide an opportunity like this only to allow us to fail? Why?*

None of it made sense.

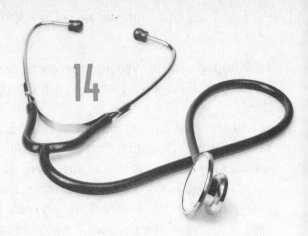

Another Set of Twins – from Zambia

For the next two and a half years, Ben continued to wonder why.

Then, in December 1996, Dr. Sam Mokgokong contacted him again. The Medical University of South Africa at Medunsa wanted to present Ben with an honorary doctorate. Ben and Candy planned to fly to South Africa the following June for him to receive that honor.

That spring, before their trip, Dr. Mokgokong called again. Another set of craniopagus Siamese twins had been born recently in Zambia. The doctors there had contacted Dr. Mokgokong to ask about the possibility of separating Joseph and Luka Banda. Dr. Mokgokong had flown to Zambia to examine the twins himself, and he felt they were good prospects for a successful separation.

He told Ben, "The Zambian government would like you and your wife to come to their country. While you are in Africa they'd like you to examine these twins and see if you think they are candidates for surgery."

Ben and Candy made arrangements to go to Zambia upon leaving South Africa. And Ben began to think, *This is amazing. Yet another set of craniopagus Siamese twins. Less than ten years after the Binder twins.*

Dr. Mokgokong took Ben and Candy on a quick tour of the hospital and introduced them to old and new friends. Ben realized things had changed since his last visit. Dr. Mokgokong proudly told them about the many lives saved by the equipment the hospital had acquired for the failed surgery on the little girls. Ben was reminded once again that God is able to take even sad experiences and use them for good.

Ben had already received eighteen honorary degrees from other colleges and universities. But he was proud and honored that the Medical University of South Africa at Medunsa awarded him a doctor of medical science.

From the time Candy and Ben began planning the trip, they had anticipated a second highlight of their visit to South Africa. They would go on a safari at Kruger National Park, a day's drive north of Medunsa.

The night before the safari, Ben prayed. He reminded God that he and Candy had only one day to visit the park. And Ben told the Lord that he would be grateful if they could see a lot of wildlife in the short time they were there. Ben never dreamed just how literally that prayer would be answered.

During the safari, their group saw all the animals they had hoped and expected to see: lions, elephants, giraffes, zebras, and many more. They also spotted rare species of snakes, such as green mambas and black mambas. Their guide told them he couldn't remember ever having another day like it. He said he saw things he'd witnessed only a few times in all his years of working in the park.

At one point, the guide pulled their four-wheel-drive Land Rover to a halt right in the middle of a roaming troop of baboons. Looking around at the fascinating but loud and rowdy creatures surrounding them, Ben recalled a television special he had seen about baboons. He had learned that an adult baboon's jaws were powerful enough to bite through a human skull. And Ben knew how strong a human skull was!

He calmly asked the driver if they really should stop right there. The guide smiled and confidently told the group that these wild animals would never bother them.

Someone had forgotten to tell the animals. Suddenly, the entire troop of baboons began climbing onto the all-terrain vehicle. A couple of the bolder ones scrambled up on the roof, dropped down through the sunroof, and landed right in the Land Rover.

Fortunately, a quick-thinking Dr. Mokgokong tossed out several slices of sandwich bread he had brought along for a picnic. The baboons leaped out of the vehicle to grab the free snack, and the guide sped away to safety.

* * *

When Ben and Candy arrived in Zambia, Dr. T. K. Lambart, Zambia's only neurosurgeon, met them at the airport and drove them to the children's hospital to meet the Banda brothers.

Like the Binder twins, Joseph and Luka Banda appeared to be healthy — a promising sign. Doctors had tested them to make certain both boys had functioning hearts, lungs, stomachs, livers, and kidneys. Unlike the South African girls, all the boys' major systems seemed to work normally and independently.

Joseph and Luka had been eating well and developing right on schedule. They could cry, smile, and reach out to grasp nearby objects. They kicked and squirmed with energy and enthusiasm. They would certainly have rolled over if only they could have turned in the same direction at the same time.

These little boys had only one significant problem: they were attached to each other at the top of their heads.

Ben looked at the way their heads were joined and wondered, *How much have their two brains been pressed together? How much are they interconnected?* He carefully examined the twins' heads, feeling along the length of their skulls' junction. He tried to imagine what problems he and the other surgeons would find inside. Then, while turning the boys gently back and forth, Ben thought of a way to answer some of his questions before he did the surgery.

Months earlier, some researchers from the Johns Hopkins radiology department had invited Ben to their laboratory for a fascinating demonstration. Working with researchers from the National University of Singapore, they were developing a three-dimensional visual-imaging system. They hoped the program could be used by surgeons to practice virtual-reality operations on a computer.

After the researchers demonstrated the idea, they asked Ben for suggestions. Ben told them he would think about it. Now, months later, in a hospital on another continent, Ben saw a way to use the technology.

During the next few months, Dr. Lambart and Dr. Mokgokong gathered all the data needed: CAT scans, angiograms, and MRIs. The researchers fed the information into their computers. Then, at Johns Hopkins in Baltimore, Ben put on a special pair of 3-D glasses and practiced the surgery on the two babies in Zambia. This new technology enabled Ben to "see" inside the heads of two little Siamese twins who were actually lying in a hospital on another continent.

He could see and study the twins' brains before he actually cut into the scalp and began the procedure in the operating room. He could spot danger areas in advance.

With the Binder twins and the Makwaeba twins, the worst part of the surgery had been sorting out the overlapping and interconnected blood vessels. Ben had to slowly and carefully separate and close off each tiny blood vessel. Being able to see and study the blood vessels ahead of time was an incredible advantage.

When Ben boarded the plane to South Africa in December 1997, he felt confident. He had planned the surgery for six months. The Banda twins had grown stronger and were now in Medunsa.

On the plane, Ben reviewed his case notes one more

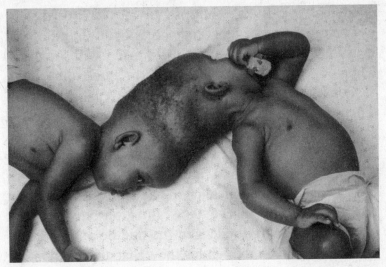

Joseph and Luka Banda.

time. Then he leaned his head back and prayed. He had done everything he could do.

Ben arrived in South Africa late Sunday afternoon. Dr. Mokgokong met his flight and took Ben right to the hospital where they examined their young patients and spoke to the boys' mother.

Most of the next day, December 29, Ben was busy meeting and getting acquainted with the surgical team. Several had participated in the unsuccessful surgery on the Makwaeba girls back in 1994. Together, the doctors and nurses reviewed the Banda case.

That night Ben spent a long time in meditation and prayer. He thanked God for the blessings of that day and asked for strength and wisdom for what was to come.

He had told Luka's and Joseph's mother, "If you will say your prayers tonight, and you ask your families and everyone you know to pray, I promise I will say mine. Then none of us will have to worry as much tomorrow."

For several hours that night, Ben prayed for the twins. Then, one last time, he looked over the angiograms (a visualization of the blood vessels after they have been injected with a radioactive substance). The Banda babies shared a large, abnormal sinus (a channel through which blood flows). The surgical team had planned to give that entire sinus to one of the twins. But after praying about it, Ben decided to divide it in the middle and give half to each twin even though he knew that approach might cause more swelling, bleeding, and perhaps even death.

The surgery on the Binder babies had required a great deal of blood. The surgery on the Makwaeba sisters had taken even more. If he split the sinus, that might cause even more bleeding and the need for yet more blood.

Still, Ben was strongly convinced that he should try to divide the shared sinus along the midpoint. But he wondered, *What will happen if I take a chance on this new, untried strategy?*

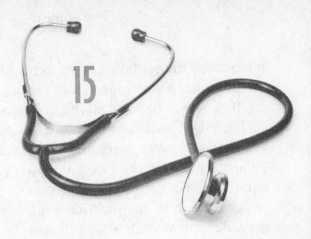

An Impossible Operation

The next day, Ben and Dr. Mokgokong arrived in the operating room before dawn. The rest of the medical team was already there. They had a pre-operation prayer meeting under a large banner that stretched across one wall declaring, "GOD BLESS JOSEPH AND LUKA." They even sang gospel songs.

When the prayer session ended, everyone got busy. The babies were prepped, draped, positioned, and put to sleep. Then the plastic surgeons spent a lot of time practicing the turning of the twins back and forth from one side to the other.

The surgery began at 6:30 a.m. Someone turned on a stereo that played the classical music Ben had requested. Activity quieted down.

The plastic surgeons removed the scalp expanders and stretched the excess skin back. Four neurosurgeons surrounded the operating table. Ben asked Dr. Lambart, the Zambian neurosurgeon and the boys' primary doctor, if he would like to drill the first burr hole.

Then Ben used ronjeurs — a special type of clipper — to snip away the bone. He proceeded very slowly. Others controlled the bleeding by treating all the raw bone edges with purified beeswax.

As a result of his practice with virtual-reality surgery, Ben already knew how the two boys' brains came together. Using scissors, he cut through the dura, the membrane covering the brains. This part of the surgery took several hours. Ben carefully clipped the many blood vessels, all in the right order, stopping to control the bleeding as he worked.

As each blood vessel was cut and closed off, the doctors took great care to watch the brains for swelling. At one point, the doctors encountered a group of blood vessels that looked like a huge tangled ball of spaghetti. They decided to leave that challenge until later.

The neurosurgeons sewed the skin flap closed over the area. Then the plastic surgeons turned the babies over. They had to prepare the skin and drape the twins again so that the doctors could begin the same procedure on the opposite side.

While that was being done, the neurosurgeons had time to sit down in a nearby conference room and eat. They watched what was happening in the operating room via closed-circuit video. They discussed what they had done so far and agreed on what to do next. Dr. Mokgokong said to Ben, "I cannot believe how

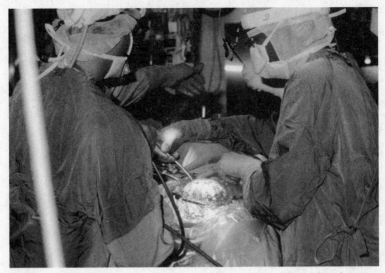

Dr. Carson in surgery.

meticulous you are with each blood vessel." Ben believed such care was important. Remarkably, so far there had been little blood loss.

The doctors spent all afternoon and into the evening repeating what they had already done on the other side of the boys' heads. The major difference on this second side was the abnormal sinus Ben had prayed about the night before. He went ahead with the unusual approach he had decided on earlier. He used clips to pinch the sinus closed. That helped control the bleeding. He cut the sinus along the midline.

Over the next few hours, the clips held and bleeding remained minimal. That part of the surgery went better than anyone had expected.

Finally, Ben was ready to tackle a second area that looked like a *small* pile of spaghetti. It took several hours to separate those entangled blood vessels. When that was finished, the second side was complete.

It was time to go back to the first side and the larger pile of spaghetti-like blood vessels. But there was a problem. The surgeons now were more tired than when they first looked at the area.

Ben felt exhausted and discouraged. He had been operating for nineteen hours. At home in the operating room at Johns Hopkins, Ben would have used a powerful $350,000 operating microscope to see the tiny blood vessels. All he had at Medunsa was a simple pair of loupe magnifying glasses and his headlight.

Ben needed a break. While the plastic surgery team was turning the boys one more time so Ben could do the next step from a different angle, Ben collapsed in a chair in the conference room. He called in the medical personnel who weren't needed then in the operating room. They discussed the operation and shared ideas. Everyone looked defeated. He wondered if they should close the wounds and give the boys and the medical team a chance to recover and regain the strength needed to go on.

"Perhaps we should consider stopping the operation at this point," Ben said. "What do you think?"

Everyone agreed on what they should do — and that was to *not* stop. They told Ben they didn't think they could keep the boys alive if they were just partially separated. They had to go on or the boys would die.

As they walked back down the hall to the operating room, Ben prayed desperately, *God, please take over and simply use me to accomplish what only you can do.*

Ben recalled two Bible verses he had read just the night before. In John 14:12–13, Jesus made a promise to his followers: "I tell you the truth, anyone who has faith in me will do what I have been doing. He will do even greater things than these, because I am going to the Father. And I will do whatever you ask in my name, so that the Son may bring glory to the Father."

So Ben stood over those babies on the operating table and prayed in Jesus' name that God would simply take over the operation. He kept praying as he began to work on the large "pile of spaghetti."

Ben's hands were now steady. He felt calm — almost as if he were just watching his hands move and someone else had actually taken over the surgery.

One after another, more than a hundred interconnected blood vessels were isolated, separated, and clipped off or reconnected. When Ben separated the last vein connecting Joseph and Luka, the stereo system began playing the "Hallelujah Chorus" from Handel's *Messiah*. Everyone in the operating room knew that something remarkable had just taken place.

Twenty-five hours of surgery had passed. But there was still no time to relax. Now the operating tables were quickly pulled apart, and the doctors immediately divided into two teams of surgeons — one team for each twin.

They still had a lot of work to do. All the neurosurgeons, despite their fatigue, were jubilant. Neither brain showed serious swelling, and there had been little blood loss. They had used less than four units of blood for the entire operation.

Even more encouraging, there wasn't swelling in any of the blood vessels. That meant circulation in both brains began successfully and everything was working well. There seemed to be every reason to believe Joseph and Luka had not only survived the surgery but that both boys might actually wake up to live full and completely normal lives.

Everyone in the operating room was excited as they finished their work. When the separation was finally done, the neurosurgeons retreated once more to the conference room where they fell asleep sitting in chairs.

Soon after the plastic surgeons completed their work, Ben returned to the operating room. As he looked at the twins, one opened his eyes and with both hands gripped the endotracheal tube sticking out of his mouth and tried to pull it out. By the time the boys reached the intensive care unit, the other twin was doing the same thing. After twenty-eight hours of surgery, this was astounding!

Congratulatory phone calls from all over the country flooded the hospital switchboard. The entire surgical team had to be escorted across the campus for a last-minute press conference. The outdoor courtyards were packed with students and hospital staff singing and dancing in a massive celebration of joy. Everyone wanted to shake the doctors' hands or pat their backs.

The press conference was jammed with television and radio reporters who had been at the hospital covering the story since the surgery began the previous morning. They had been filing hourly updates to their stations throughout the country. The story of the Banda boys had fascinated people in South Africa. Now it seemed as though the entire country wanted to celebrate the wonderful accomplishment.

Ben spent a few minutes answering reporters' questions, then the other doctors took a turn. Hospital officials made official statements. Even the boys' mother, now a very happy woman, made an appearance.

The Zambian ambassador delivered his country's official thanks to everyone involved, stating that the Zambian people, along with the president and first lady, had been praying. He invited Ben and the other surgeons to a thanksgiving dinner celebration the next day in the Zambian embassy.

Unfortunately, Ben's flight home was scheduled to leave later that evening. He expected to be home in Maryland by the time the Zambian ambassador served the main course. Ben hated to miss the celebration, but in truth he was looking forward to collapsing in his own bed.

When Dr. Mokgokong dropped him off at his hotel, Ben noticed that something was wrong — the hotel was dark and no one seemed to be inside. He rang the bell at the front desk and waited. Nothing happened.

Suddenly, a policewoman appeared at the front door. When she spotted Ben inside, she was surprised. "How did you get in?" she wanted to know.

"I walked in the front door," Ben told her. "I'm a guest here."

"That's impossible," she said, looking at Ben suspiciously. "The hotel is closed for the holiday."

"Closed? I didn't know," Ben said. "I left early yesterday morning and didn't return last night. I've been in surgery for twenty-eight hours, and I just want to get a little sleep. I need to at least collect my luggage. I have to catch a flight out of the country tonight."

The officer smiled broadly. "You're that American doctor who operated on the Siamese twins, aren't you?" She quickly called the hotel's owner. He rushed over, gave Ben his room key, and promised to personally see that no one disturbed him until he needed to leave for the airport.

A couple of weeks after returning home, Ben received word that the Banda boys were amazing their doctors. They were already beginning to crawl, an activity that had been physically impossible before the surgery. Ben knew then that those two little boys were on their way to full and normal lives.

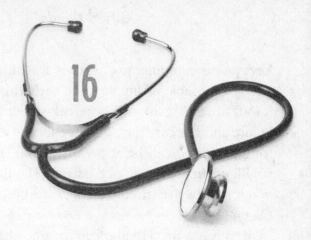

Cancer

Lunchtime. Ben munched on an apple from the brown-bag lunch Candy had handed him as he'd rushed out the door before six that morning. He sorted through a tall stack of medical folders one of his assistants had placed on his desk. The phone rang for the third time in fifteen minutes. The first two calls had eaten away half of his twenty-minute lunch break, and he had to be back down in the operating room in five minutes for his next case. He'd decided to let his voice mail pick up the call when his office manager stuck her head in the door. "You may want to take this one. It's that television reporter you promised to fit in today. She wants to talk to you about the surgery on those Nepalese twins in Singapore last month."

Ben picked up the receiver. "This is Dr. Carson." He listened, told the reporter, "Hold on," and tapped a few

keys on his computer to check his schedule. "I think so...
I've got a couple of shunts to do early this afternoon, but
it looks like I'll have a short break sometime around 3:30
before another case that will probably go until 7:00 or 8:00
tonight. If you can be at my office and set up by 3:15 or
so, I'll get here as soon as possible. I should be able to give
you ten or twelve minutes. That's the best I can do today.
Okay?"

Ben hung up. He glanced around the office. Stacks
of medical files and large envelopes containing X-ray,
MRI, and CAT scan film covered the surface of a small
conference table, one upholstered chair, and most of a
couch. He shook his head, stood up, grabbed the rest of
his apple, and headed out the door toward the stairs to
the operating room.

After all the media coverage of his first conjoined
twins case, the Binder boys, Ben had assured Candy that
life would settle down again. But it never did. What he'd
been so sure was a once-in-a-lifetime opportunity led to
a line of challenging cases, each bringing him more publicity and worldwide recognition. All the international
attention surrounding the Banda case had thrust Ben
back into the public eye.

Newspapers and magazines published countless stories about him. Radio and television reporters called
to ask for interviews. He felt like he'd had more than
enough press coverage to last a lifetime, but he knew the
publicity was good for the hospital. And the growing
reputation of the Johns Hopkins Pediatric Neurosurgical

Department brought in more interesting and challenging cases.

* * *

All this unexpected publicity helped nourish another dream of Ben's — an ambitious dream that had been born as he traveled the country speaking to students. In every school he visited, Ben noticed display cases in the hallways, filled with trophies of all shapes and sizes for every sport. He thought about how American culture makes heroes of athletes and entertainers.

He wondered, *What if every elementary, middle, and high school in America gave the same sort of recognition to academic achievers as they do to athletes? What if students began looking up to scholars as heroes too?*

To help make that happen, Ben and Candy started the Carson Scholars Fund to recognize and promote young people (starting as young as fourth grade) for superior academic achievement and for service to others in their communities. Not only are Carson scholars honored each year at big regional banquets, receiving nice awards to take home, but they are recognized in front of their peers at their schools. Each scholar's name is engraved on an award and placed in the school trophy case. In addition, each one receives a thousand-dollar scholarship to use for college.

So far the Carson Scholars organization has awarded almost six thousand scholarships totaling nearly $6 million to young scholars from all fifty states. Ben and Candy continue to dream that one day every school in

America will participate in an annual Carson Scholars program. (To learn how your school can get involved, go to the website: *www.carsonscholars.org.*)

Only a couple of years after the successful surgery on the Banda boys, a surgeon in Singapore had asked for Ben's help in the case of eleven-month-old craniopagus twin girls from Nepal. Ben consulted and worked long-distance through the use of a computer's virtual workstation to assist in the operation that took ninety-plus hours and successfully separated these babies. But the biggest impact of such high-profile cases went beyond rare cases of conjoined twins; the publicity also impacted Ben and his entire department. Because of the growing reputation of its most famous neurosurgeon, Johns Hopkins became the hospital of choice for more and more parents of children with rare and serious neurological conditions.

The average number of surgeries done by an American neurosurgeon is approximately 150 per year. Ben was performing 450 operations a year. But as the piles of files in his office indicated, he was in danger of being overwhelmed by the demands of seeing all the patients scheduled for follow-up visits. The surgical load became so heavy that he often started before 7:00 a.m. and didn't finish in the operating room until late at night. Twice, after long, exhausting days in surgery, Ben fell asleep at the wheel on the drive home. He vowed to hire more staff and reduce his surgical workload.

An even more serious experience in 2002 prompted Ben to further examine both his personal and professional priorities. When he noticed some telltale physical symptoms, Ben had a blood test taken. When these results showed a slightly high level of specific antigens in his blood, his doctor suggested a biopsy of his prostate to rule out the possibility of cancer.

Ben asked the colleague who would test the sample to call him as soon as he got the results. The next day, while Ben was in surgery, the doctor called the OR and a nurse held the receiver up to Ben's ear.

That's how Ben got the bad news. Not only did he have prostate cancer, but the biopsy showed it was a very aggressive form. It would be a tough fight for survival. Somehow Ben put that out of his mind and successfully completed his operation.

Not until he was driving home did it hit him. *Wow! My life may not be as long as I thought it would be!* He began to think of all the people he would leave behind: Candy, his three sons, his mother, his colleagues, and his patients. Saddened, he thought too of all the plans he had made, all the things he'd started that he might not finish.

Ben was scheduled for an MRI, a high-resolution image of his entire body, to determine whether the cancer had metastasized (spread elsewhere in his body). If it hadn't, he would be a good candidate for surgery to remove the cancer.

The MRI was done at Johns Hopkins. When Ben came out of the MRI machine, one of the technicians handed him an envelope with copies of his scans. Ben carried the sheets of film back to his office and stuck the first one up on the lighted scan board hanging on his wall. His heart sank as he spotted a series of suspicious spots up and down the spine. He wasn't a radiologist, but he'd seen enough scans over the years to know this one looked very, very bad for the patient. Instinctively, just to be sure, he double-checked the identification on the border of the film: "Patient: Carson, Ben."

He sank down in his desk chair. *I really am going to die from this.*

Somehow the word got out. The next day an area radio station reported that Ben had been diagnosed with cancer — a malignant brain tumor, they said. A flurry of follow-up reports in the local media claimed it was lung cancer, or colon cancer, or pancreatic cancer, or kidney cancer.

Some reports said he was dying. Or he had already died. One woman called Ben's office. "I heard Dr. Carson is dead! I want to speak to him!" For three days running, major articles appeared in the *Washington Post.*

Ben tried to ignore all the commotion. He didn't even glance at the newspaper when he got up early on the Fourth of July to take a long, quiet walk alone around his farm in the early-morning light. He noticed how especially beautiful and peaceful everything looked. He heard the birds singing and thought, *I've really taken so much for granted in my life. I need to take more time to enjoy all these wonderful things God has created.* He had always wondered how he would react when he faced death. Now he knew; he felt an amazing sense of peace.

All of a sudden, very few things mattered. He began to appreciate life more. He began to appreciate his loved

The Carson family at home: Ben, Murray, Rhoeyce, Candy, and BJ.

ones more. He began to appreciate God much more. He kept reassuring himself and those closest to him: *God doesn't make mistakes. So if I'm supposed to die, there must be a very good reason for it. I'm not going to question God. It's okay.* Still, the thought of leaving his family was difficult.

On a positive note, the public support and concern nearly overwhelmed Ben. In the wake of his diagnosis, he received mailbags full of cards and letters from across the globe — from janitors who worked in the hospital, from families of former patients, from students who said they had read his books and written book reports on them in school, even a letter from the president and first lady of the United States — all saying they were praying for him. He told people, "I believe God is listening to all those prayers. In fact, I suspect he's getting tired of hearing about me."

Six days after the MRI, after many consultations with experts and several second opinions, Ben received wonderful news. The abnormal spots that showed up on the scan of his spine and looked like cancerous lesions were just minor abnormalities in his bone marrow — a rare though harmless condition he'd been born with.

The cancer had not metastasized. Ben had prostate surgery to successfully remove the cancer. And his doctor predicted a long, full life.

Today, Ben says he still takes time every day to listen to the birds sing and to appreciate the beauty around him. "But it's not just nature that I have a deeper appreciation for. My own cancer experience has resulted in added understanding for my patients and greater empathy for all that their families are going through. It has also given me a greater appreciation for all the people in my life. If anything, it has given me a deeper sense of dependency on and trust in God as well. It certainly has made me more determined than ever to wisely and carefully consider the use of my time and expertise to help others."

All of that helps to explain why, the following year, he got involved in the most difficult case of his entire career.

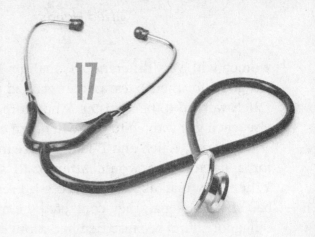

The Bijani Twins: Ben's Toughest Case Yet

In 2003, the same medical team from Singapore invited Ben to help separate another set of conjoined twins. Ben declined. Even though the Bijani sisters were the most interesting case Ben had ever encountered, he didn't believe surgery would be successful. The risk was too great.

This pair of Iranian twins had surprised their doctors not only by living to the age of twenty-nine but by managing a number of impressive accomplishments. They had learned to walk and had attended school with their peers, eventually graduating from college and then law school. That final accomplishment was now the source of increased tension between them.

The sisters had spent their entire lives attached at the side of the head, never able to be alone. Even going to the bathroom meant a joint decision. Now these two young women with very different personalities had very different goals for their lives. Ladan wanted to be a lawyer. Laleh wanted to be a writer. And more than anything else, each girl wanted to make her own choice.

For years, Laleh and Ladan had searched the world for a doctor who would attempt to separate them. When they read about the successful separation of the babies from Nepal, they contacted the medical team in Singapore. And because Ben had more experience with such surgeries than anyone else in the world, they specifically asked that he be involved with their operation.

Though he was honored by their request, Ben turned down the invitation. He was concerned the surgery would be very different and far more dangerous than any of his previous cases. The Bijani sisters were adults, not children. They did not have young and adaptable brains like all the other patients he'd tried to separate. In his opinion, the chance of surviving was not good.

Plus, the sisters were healthy and had already adapted well for their twenty-nine years together. Ben worried that even if they survived physically, the emotional adjustment of separation might be more than they could handle.

But the more Ben learned about the Bijanis, the more he rethought his decision. Unlike his younger patients, the sisters understood the risk of surgery and could make the decision for themselves. It bothered him to learn that they were having trouble getting along with each other because of the tension over their differing career desires. (He could only imagine how frustrating it must be for the sisters to get angry and argue with each other and never be able to walk away from the conflict and be alone.) Both women insisted they would rather have the surgery and face the possibility of dying than go on living the way they were, with no chance for independent lives.

When it became clear the Bijanis were determined to proceed with plans for the operation, whether or not Ben agreed to join the surgical team, Ben decided he would assist after all. He didn't want to see them die and wonder for the rest of his life if his expertise and experience (more experience with craniopagus twin cases than any other surgeon in the world) might have made a difference.

After months of long-distance consulting and computer modeling, Ben flew to Singapore and finally met the Bijanis at the hospital the day before their scheduled surgery. He could not have been more impressed with the sisters. Although their skulls were fused above and behind their ears (over an area half the size of a head), so that their faces turned permanently away from each other at a 130-degree angle, they did a remarkable job of moving around. With their ears touching, their inside shoulders and arms constantly rubbing, they were forced to lean their upper bodies toward one another and drop their inside shoulders to create room to move and keep their balance. They walked up to shake hands with Ben, gracefully turned through a doorway, and sat down together on a couch to talk with him.

Laleh and Ladan were bright, well-spoken, warm, friendly, and brave—and very determined to go through with the operation. Ben told them once more the odds were not good. They assured him they understood the risk and insisted again that more than anything they wanted a chance to live normal, separate lives. Ben assured them the team could not be better prepared. He promised them he would do everything he could to ensure a successful surgery the next day. Finally, Ben told them what he always said to his patients (and their parents) prior to surgery: "I've never known a case yet where worry helped. So I'm going to say my prayers tonight before I go to sleep. I hope you'll do the same. I believe if we do that, we'll all have less to worry about tomorrow."

Twenty-eight physicians and more than a hundred nurses, technicians, and assistants crowded into the operating room to participate in the surgery the next morning. The group of newspaper, radio, and television reporters waiting outside the hospital seemed even larger.

Inside the operating room, tension grew as hours passed. This was indeed the most challenging case Ben had ever faced. As they slowly began to separate the connected tissue and divide areas where blood drained from the brain, Ben suddenly realized the blood had spontaneously established new circulatory pathways. While that was good in the sense it meant the brain was adapting and getting the blood it needed, it also meant the doctors had no idea where these new blood vessels were going. The circulatory map they had memorized after studying the sisters' CAT scans and MRIs for the past few months was changing before their eyes. Now no one knew exactly what the blood was doing or where it was going inside the twins' brains.

After thirty-two hours, Ben strongly recommended they stop the surgery, reposition the skull pieces they had cut away, sew the women back up, and take time to study the new circulation patterns. Then they could go back in and attempt the separation again, perhaps in stages, to give the brains a chance to adapt.

But this wasn't Johns Hopkins; Ben was not in charge.

Not until that moment did Ben learn that the doctors who *were* in charge had promised the Bijani sisters that once they started the surgery, there would be no stopping or turning back. Laleh and Ladan had insisted they would wake up separated or not at all.

So the operation went on. Slowly, the surgical team carefully separated Ladan's and Laleh's brains. Ben's hands and fingers began to cramp; he felt the muscles tighten across the back of his neck and shoulders. But after fifty hours, he began to sense new hope and a happy ending for two very special and brave young women.

Ninety percent of the brain surfaces were separated, and the patients remained stable. Everything looked good.

Some of the last bits to cut and clip were located in the hardest place to reach — in the back, down below the ears, where the doctors had left one final spot of fused bone to stabilize the base of the skulls and hold the two women together.

Unfortunately, the difficult angle wasn't the only problem they encountered. The doctors discovered where all the new blood channels were now draining.

Every time they clipped off one bleeder in the area, another would start. For two hours, Ben and his colleagues battled to stem the flow of blood. Just when it looked as if they were gaining ground, Ladan's heart quit beating.

The doctors had no choice but to cut the twins apart immediately. Ben and one of the other surgeons continued work to control Laleh's bleeding, while another team tried desperately, but unsuccessfully, to revive her sister. After Ladan died, everyone concentrated on saving Laleh. But ninety minutes later, she died from uncontrollable blood loss.

After fifty-three hours of surgery, with only three or four one-hour catnaps, Ben wasn't sure which sensation cut deeper—his sadness or his fatigue. He just knew it was a terrible feeling he never wanted to experience again.

The media broadcast the tragic news around the world. Immediately, some questioned the decision to operate—asking if the surgery had really been worth the risk. When one doubtful reporter asked Ben how he felt about the "failure" of the operation, Ben talked about his feelings of respect and fondness for the Bijani twins, and his great sadness over their deaths. But he also added, "It's a *failure* only if no good comes out of it. Thomas Edison said he had to discover 999 ways a lightbulb would not work; yet we have lights today. I believe a day will come when twins such as these can have a normal life and a safe separation. And I think Ladan and Laleh will have contributed significantly to those individuals in the future who will be able to enjoy what the dream of these two courageous young ladies was—to live normal, independent lives."

Ben still had some unanswered questions, just as he did after the deaths of the Makwaeba twins back in South Africa. But he'd learned some important lessons in the years between those cases. He now had enough faith to believe there were answers to his questions and he knew those answers would become clear as time went on.

Those were crucial lessons Ben felt needed to be shared with others.

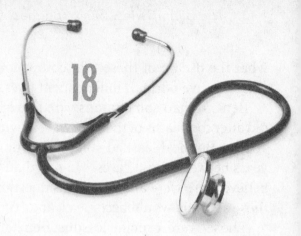

Do You Have a Brain?

Almost every week, Benjamin Solomon Carson travels somewhere to speak. And like his namesake, King Solomon (author of the biblical book of Proverbs), Ben freely shares with others the wisdom he's gained and the invaluable lessons he's learned.

Ben is a popular speaker, and people have to invite him months, sometimes years, in advance. He has spoken in school assemblies, for college graduations, at business conventions, in church services, in arenas filled with thousands of people. In 1997 Ben was even invited to be the keynote speaker at the National Prayer Breakfast in Washington, D.C., where he shared his life story and talked about his personal faith in God in front of the President of the United States, the President's Cabinet, most of Congress, several justices of the Supreme Court, and thousands of other leaders from around the country and the world. Ben considered that opportunity a great honor.

But his favorite audience is young people. Many Monday mornings during the school year, Ben hosts 700 to 800 students from the Baltimore-area schools who visit Johns Hopkins on educational field trips. Ben meets with students in Turner Auditorium, where he shows slides about neurosurgery, Siamese twins, and many other things that take place at Johns Hopkins.

Wherever Ben talks to young people, he introduces himself as a former "class dummy" who became the director of pediatric neurosurgery at one of the greatest medical institutions in the world. He points to himself as living proof that with education and God's help, anything is possible. And he always explains how reading turned his life around, provided an escape from poverty, and helped his dreams to come true.

He tells students that it doesn't matter who they are, what color their skin is, where they come from, or how much money their family has. Education is the great equalizer. For example, to become a licensed physician he needed one thing — the required education. It didn't matter that his family was poor. Education and determination were all he needed to fulfill his dream of becoming a doctor.

He warns against one of the most dangerous things students can face and confesses how it nearly ruined his own life. He spells it out, "P-E-E-R-S! That stands for People who Encourage Errors, Rudeness, and Stupidity. And that's just what my negative peers did for me."

Ben challenges his listeners to use the mind God gave each of them to think for themselves and to figure out how to overcome the challenges they face.

Ben always tries to inspire his audience by talking about the amazing potential of the human brain. Here again he uses his own experience as an example:

"As boys, whenever my brother, Curtis, and I would offer an excuse to our mother as an explanation for why we failed to accomplish something she asked or expected us to do, anytime we complained about some seemingly insurmountable problem, anytime we grew weary or became discouraged by some obstacle in the road of life, and especially if we ever whined about anything, Mother always offered a standard response. She would get this puzzled look on her face and ask, 'Do you have a brain?'

"The implication was crystal clear: If you have a brain, use it! It's all you need to overcome any problem life presents.

"My mother instilled in us a deep respect for the potential of the human brain, and for me that respect has deepened over the years to an attitude I can only describe as *awe*. Every time I open a child's head and see a brain, I marvel at the mystery. *This* is what makes every one of us who we are. *This* is what holds all our memories, all our thoughts, all our dreams. *This* is what makes us different from each other in millions of ways. And yet, if I could expose my brain and expose your brain, and place them side by side, you wouldn't be able to tell the difference—even though we might be very different people. That still amazes me.

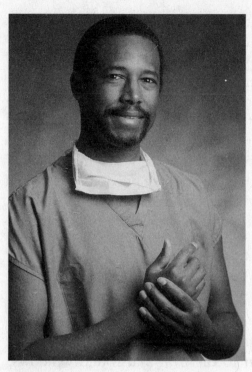

Dr. Ben Carson.

"Inside each human brain are billions and billions of complex interconnections and neurons and synapses, which science has only barely begun to understand. When you throw on top of that the related phenomena of mind and spirit, the human brain becomes a laboratory so vast and intricate, you could work in it for a millennium and hardly scratch the surface.

"Do you realize that no supercomputer on earth can come close to the capacity of the average human brain? This resource each one of us has is a tremendous gift from God—the most complex organ system in the entire universe. Your brain can take in two million bits of information per second. If I could bring one person up onstage, have her look out at this crowd for one second, and lead her away, fifty years later I could perform an operation, take off the cranial bone, put in some depth electrodes, stimulate the appropriate area of her brain, and she could not only remember where each of you was sitting but what all eight hundred of you were wearing. That's how amazing and complex the human brain is. It's truly mind-boggling."

To further illustrate this, Ben will ask the students in his audience various questions, such as, how many remember what they had for breakfast that morning? Or how many recall what they did the previous afternoon? The point is to get them to raise their hands.

Then he will run through a rapid-fire riff something like this:

"Do you know what your brain had to do when I asked that question? First, the sound waves had to leave my lips, travel through the air into your external auditory meatus, travel down to your tympanic membrane, and set up a vibratory force that traveled across the ossicles of your middle ear to the oval and round windows, generating a vibratory force in the endolymph, which mechanically distorts the microcilia, converting mechanical energy to electrical energy, which traveled across the cochlear nerve to the cochlear nucleus at the pontomedullary junction, from there to the superior olivary nucleus, ascending bilaterally up the brain stem through the lateral lemniscus to the inferior colliculus and the medial geniculate nucleus, then across the thalamic radiations to the posterior temporal lobes to begin the auditory processing, from there to the frontal lobes, coming down the tract of Vicq d'Azyr, retrieving the memory from the medial hippocampal structures and the mammillary bodies, back to the frontal lobes to start the motor response at the Betz cell level, coming down the corticospinal tract, across the internal capsule into the cerebral peduncle, descending to the cervicomedullary decussation into the spinal cord gray matter, synapsing, and going out to the neuromuscular junction, stimulating the nerve and the muscle so you could raise your hand." The crowd never fails to break into applause before Ben goes on to add ...

"Of course, that's the simplified version. If I had included all the inhibitory and coordinating influences, we would be talking for hours about this one thing.

"Did you know your brain can do all that and you barely have to think about it? And it can be doing multiple, more complicated things simultaneously. So tell me ... with a brain like that, why would anyone ever utter the words *I can't*?

"We can complain about the problems we face in life, we can try to ignore them, we can allow ourselves to be paralyzed by the obstacles we see. Or we can ask ourselves my mother's question: Do we each have a brain? Then let's use this incredible tool God has given us!"

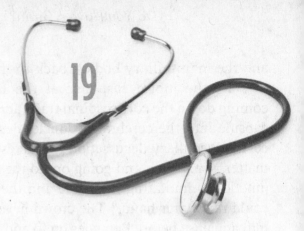

Thinking Big

Ben often challenges listeners of all ages to "think big." He tells audiences that "think big" is his philosophy for success in life. And he uses the letters that spell out the words to make his points:

"The T is for talent," Ben says, "which God gives to every individual. Not just the ability to sing and dance and throw a ball. Very few people are talented at basketball. Only seven out of every million basketball players are good enough to play in the NBA. But all of us are good at something. We just have to think about it and ask ourselves these questions: What have I done well so far in life? What school subjects am I good at? What do I do that other people compliment me for? What do I think is fun to do that my friends think is work?

"These are your talents. When I was deciding what to do with my life, I had to spend time analyzing myself. I asked, What is it that I really ought to be doing? What am I really good at? That's how I came up with the idea to go into neurosurgery.

"The H—in THINK BIG—is for honesty. One of my classmates at Yale graduated magna cum laude. That means he made very, very high grades. But he was not honest. He often broke rules. He cheated on exams. Our tests were based on the honor code. Professors would hand out the test questions and leave the room. They trusted that we would not look up the answers in our books. But during exams, I often saw this student open his book. He must have thought, *The professor isn't here to see me. The other students can see me cheat, but they don't matter.* Honesty does matter. Of all my fellow classmates who applied to go to medical school, he was the only one who was not accepted.

"The I is for insight, which comes from listening to people who have already been where you are trying to go. Solomon, the wisest man who ever lived, said, 'Wise is the man who can learn from someone else's triumphs and mistakes. The person who cannot is a fool.'

"When I was growing up, my mother worked in the homes of wealthy families. As she went about her work, Mother asked her employers questions. She noticed what they read, how they spent their time, the kinds of activities they chose. And when she noted that wealthy people did not spend much time watching television, she gained insight from that.

"The N—in THINK BIG—is for nice. Be nice to people. Once they get over their suspicions about why you're being nice, they'll almost always be nice to you. And you can get so much more done when people are being nice to you and you're nice to them.

"If you're not a nice person, I challenge you to try it for one week. What will that mean? It means not talking about people behind their backs. It means if you see somebody struggling with something, help them with it. It requires putting yourself in the other person's place before you begin to criticize.

"If the elevator door is open and there is only one space left, let someone else get on. It means greeting people. When you get in the elevator or you meet people in the hallway at school, say, 'Good morning.' Once they get over their initial shock, most people will be happy to greet you in return. You'll find that being nice is often contagious.

"The K is for knowledge, which can make you into a more valuable person. Yes, I do own a big house and drive nice cars. I have many of the things that money can buy. But are they important? Of course not. If somebody comes along and takes it all away, it's no big deal. I can get it all back using what's inside my head.

"That's what Solomon meant when he said, 'Gold is nice, silver is nice, rubies are nice. But to be treasured far above all those things are knowledge, wisdom, and understanding.' Because with knowledge, wisdom, and understanding, you can get all the gold, silver, and rubies you need. But more importantly, you come to realize that gold and silver and rubies aren't really very important. It's a far more valuable thing to develop your

God-given talents to the point where you become a blessing to the people around you.

"The B is for books—an invaluable resource for obtaining success. My own story is one of the best examples I could give you of that.

"The second I is for in-depth learning—learning for the sake of knowledge and understanding as opposed to superficial, or shallow, learning. Superficial learners are people who cram, cram, cram before a test. They may do fine on the exam, but three weeks later, they don't remember anything.

"The last letter is G—for God. We live in a society where people are always saying, 'You can't talk about God in public.' As if somehow doing so violates the concept of church and state.

"Thomas Jefferson, one of our founding fathers, had 190 religious volumes in his library. The Declaration of Independence talks about certain inalienable rights, which our Creator endows us with. The Pledge of Allegiance to our flag says we are 'one country, under God.' Almost every courtroom in the land has on its walls, 'In God We Trust.' Every coin in our pockets, every bill in our wallets, also says, 'In God We Trust.'

"If a belief in God was important enough to be cited in our Declaration of Independence, if it's proclaimed in our Pledge, if it's posted in our courts, and it's engraved on our money, we can certainly talk about it in public!

"We need to make it clear to people that it's all right to live by godly principles — loving our fellow man, caring for our neighbors, and living a life of service by developing our God-given talents so that we might be of value to the people around us. We need to remind each other there is nothing judgmental about having values and principles, and there's nothing wrong with standing for something.

"If we apply God's truths to our own lives, if we instill these biblical values in the next generation, then, and only then, will America be truly united and become the greatest nation the world has ever known."

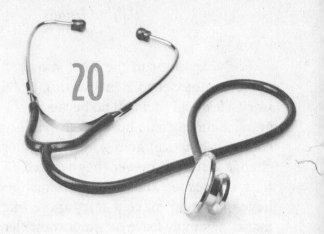

The Better/Higher Way

Ben Carson's amazing life journey — from class dummy to world-famous brain surgeon — has earned him much recognition and many impressive awards. Millions of people around the world have read his story in countless newspaper stories, magazine articles, and books. His life story has been performed onstage in a play seen by many thousands of Baltimore-area schoolchildren over the years.

In 2009, his autobiography was made into a Turner Network Television movie starring Cuba Gooding Jr. That movie, titled *Gifted Hands,* has been rerun countless times since on a variety of cable networks. And with sales approaching an astounding 500,000 and still going strong, the DVD version of Ben's story has been and will continue to be seen by millions more people all over the world.

For years prior to the TNT movie, numerous film-makers approached Ben wanting to tell his inspiring story. He'd told them all no because they wanted him to grant them "artistic license"—a Hollywood term (and common practice) giving movie studios permission to change a story however they wanted. They would add fictional scenes and characters just because they believed it would make a story more interesting or dramatic, or simply leave out important elements of a story they didn't like or that might not fit their own agenda or belief system.

Ben decided he'd rather not have his story ever made into a movie, unless the filmmakers agreed to tell the true story of his life, and to make the movie as realistic as possible in every way. Most importantly, he wanted any movie to accurately and honestly portray the significant role that Ben's faith in God had played in his personal life and his professional success. So Ben insisted he be given final say-so over the movie's accuracy, which parts of his story absolutely needed to be included, as well as what scenes and details could be left out.

The TNT moviemakers not only agreed to Ben's terms, they committed themselves to fulfilling their agreement. "One reason the surgical scenes in the movie were so true-to-life," Ben explains, "was because the studio hired real doctors, nurses, and medical technicians to play the part of the surgical team in every operating room scene. They didn't film actual surgeries; they used realistic props—including an incredibly authentic-looking brain. But the actors performing the make-believe surgery executed their roles well because they were all medical professionals."

Even so, the film crew checked with Ben constantly to ensure their accuracy to his satisfaction. "During production," recalls Ben, "I'd receive three, four, sometimes five phone calls a day from someone on the set, wanting to double-check with me about some detail or other.

"Occasionally I'd be performing surgery myself when one of their calls came through. After I'd reached a safe stopping point, I would take the call. A nurse would hold the phone up to my ear to maintain a sterile field, so I wouldn't have to leave the room, scrub in again, and put on a new set of gown and gloves. I'd speak into the phone and explain, 'I'm in the middle of brain surgery right now, can ...'"

"And more often than not they'd interrupt me to say something like this: 'That's okay, Dr. Carson. We've just got one quick question ...'"

"Hollywood always seems to have its own priorities."

And yet, when Ben and Candy Carson had the opportunity to visit the movie set during filming on location in Detroit, the entire cast and crew welcomed them enthusiastically. Cuba Gooding Jr., who starred in the movie as Ben, made a point of pulling them aside to explain the warm reception.

"You need to understand," the famous actor told the Carsons, "that for all of us working on this movie—this is not just a *job*. We consider it a *mission*!"

Clearly the inspirational message in Ben's life story and his personal testimony of faith had made an impact on the actors and filmmakers themselves. This is no doubt one reason why the finished movie is still having such a positively overwhelming response from the millions of viewers who've watched it on TV and are still seeing it on DVD.

* * *

The City of Detroit Public Schools honored one of its most famous and accomplished alumni by creating and naming one of its magnet schools the Dr. Benjamin Carson High School for Science and Medicine. As proud as it made Ben to be recognized in such a significant way in the city where he grew up, what excites him most about this school with his name on it is the hope it provides young people in Detroit today. Students who have a fascination with science and medicine will get an even better chance to pursue their goals and interests in a school dedicated to preparing them to achieve their own professional dreams.

But it's not only Detroit where Ben's achievements and example are honored. The Atlanta Public Schools have also established a middle school named the Benjamin S. Carson Honors Preparatory School and also a special Business, Engineering, Science, and Technology (B.E.S.T.) Academy at Benjamin S. Carson Educational Complex in the heart of Georgia's capital. The mission of the B.E.S.T. Academy is to develop globally competitive leaders by providing a rigorous college preparatory curriculum utilizing gender-based strategies (it's a school specifically for boys) in a safe and nurturing learning environment.

In the spring of 2012, Ben and Candy traveled to Africa for the inauguration of the Benjamin S. Carson Sr. School of Medicine and Babcock University Teaching Hospital on the outskirts of Lagos, Nigeria. As he addressed the crowd of 50,000 people who came to the university's commencement, Ben couldn't help but remember the early childhood dream he'd had about becoming a missionary doctor. "That was my life plan for a number of years," Ben says. "But God had other ideas for me. Because I followed his plan, rather than my own, I've been able to share my faith and God's great love for the world in more ways, and to have more influence on more people than I probably could have done as a missionary.

"And now here I was in Africa, opening a Christian medical school with my name on it, an institution that would train many doctors who will in turn develop their own ministry of healing throughout Africa, and hopefully around the world. Which just goes to show that God's plans for us are always better than the plans we have for ourselves. If we just read and obey his Word and follow Jesus, the Lord will surprise us and enable us to do more and greater things than we might have ever imagined on our own.

"Indeed, the Bible reminds us of this in Isaiah 55:9 where it says God's ways are higher than our ways, 'as the heavens are higher than the earth.' And my experience has proven that truth to me again and again throughout my life."

* * *

Over the years, colleges and universities around the world have granted Ben seventy-some honorary doctorates.

Each year the National Association for the Advancement of Colored People (NAACP) bestows the Spingarn Award to one person "for outstanding achievement by an African American." Former recipients include George Washington Carver, Thurgood Marshall, Jackie Robinson, Rosa Parks, Martin Luther King Jr., Bill Cosby Jr., and Colin Powell. Ben received his gold Spingarn medal in 2006 "in tribute for a lifetime of growth and singular achievement, from the bottom of his fifth grade class, to become the youngest ever Chief of Pediatric Neurosurgery in the United States."

The Lincoln Medal is also an annual award, given by Ford's Theatre in Washington, D.C., "to individuals who, through their body of work, accomplishments or personal attributes, exemplify the lasting legacy, and mettle of character embodied by the most beloved President in our Nation's history, Abraham Lincoln." In 2008, during a special White House ceremony, Ben received this honor along with civil rights activist and poet Maya Angelou; actress Ruby Dee; and the first woman ever to serve as a Supreme Court justice, Sandra Day O'Connor.

After the presentation, President George W. Bush and his wife, Laura, stayed to have pictures taken with the recipients. When they thoughtfully told Ben they would gladly pose for a picture with his mother, Sonya Carson stepped forward and said she would like a photo with just the First Lady. According to Ben, "the President laughed and exclaimed, 'I guess I've been asked to step out of the picture!' He was gracious and a good sport about it. And I guess he wasn't too offended because I was invited back to the White House again a few weeks later."

Indeed, on June 19, 2008, President George W. Bush invited the entire Carson family to a special ceremony at the White House, where he presented the Presidential Medal of Freedom, the United States' highest civilian honor, to Ben for his work as a surgeon and his efforts to improve the lives of youth. Ben says, "There was probably more pomp and circumstance at that event than anything I've experienced my entire life. We got the royal treatment at the White House with an orchestra, a color guard, military attachés, the President's Cabinet, senators, justices of the Supreme Court, and as many other dignitaries as could crowd into the room. Another incredibly humbling honor."

But what means far more to Ben Carson than all the public recognition and honors he's been given are the personal letters—hundreds of thousands—he has received from around the world. Every week, almost every day, young people write to tell Ben their lives were changed by hearing him tell his story, by reading one of his books, by seeing an interview on television or in some magazine, and realizing they each have a brain and the ability to define their own lives.

"If that's the only legacy I leave," Ben says, "I'll be happy, and my life will have been worth it."

Which is why, whenever he tells his story to young people, and especially when he talks about the many amazing surgeries he's been involved with, Ben makes a point of saying, "I know God had a hand in all these events, just as I know he has had a hand in shaping everything good in my life. Thanks to God and a courageous mother, a poor kid from the streets of Detroit has been able to take part in medical miracles. I have been blessed with a wonderful wife, three healthy boys, and a loving community of church and professional friends.

"But I want God to continue to use me to help others. I pray every day that I can be the best doctor, father, and husband possible and a caring member of my church and community.

"I feel an obligation to act as a role model for young people who feel trapped by their dismal situations. If I can't do anything else, I want to provide one living example of someone who came from a disadvantaged background and made it. Because I want other young people to realize that when you THINK BIG and ask God for his help, he will use you, and dreams can come true."

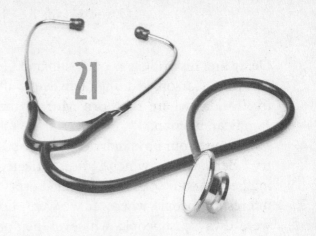

Honors, Milestones, and Plans

The message and challenge Ben feels compelled to share with young people wherever he goes—that God will direct and empower them to do great things if they trust and follow him—is a message he believes with all his heart. He's learned that truth by experiencing how God has worked in and through him throughout his entire life. And today, just as he's trusted the Lord in the past, Ben's trusting God with his future—even as he has recently reached new milestones that are prompting him to make important decisions about the rest of his life.

Some of those milestones have been personal and relatively private. Like the fact that all three of Ben and Candy's sons got married during the same year, 2011. Their second son, BJ, got married first—in Virginia to a young woman whose family came from India. The youngest Carson son, Rhoeyce, got married in

Delaware; his bride was of Syrian and German descent. The third Carson wedding of an eventful year took place in Florida, where firstborn Murray married a young Jamaican woman.

"None of our boys married anyone born in this country," Ben laughs, "which I guess reflected their upbringing because our sons have traveled everywhere and met interesting people wherever we went. For them, people were always just people, whatever their nationality, race, or background; they didn't see them any other way.

"So the fact that we had three very different international weddings was not surprising to me. It just means each of our grandchildren [the first of whom, a beautiful granddaughter, was born in 2012] will be blessed with an interesting and diverse family heritage."

* * *

For years Ben had carefully contemplated another significant milestone he realized was fast approaching. The decision required of him was not only personal but also professional, and would impact many other people whom he felt needed to know. So Ben talked with family and some of his closest colleagues and informed Johns Hopkins what he'd decided. Late in 2012, he made public his plans to retire from the practice of surgery on June 30, 2013.

Many neurosurgeons give up their work in the OR long before they reach their sixties. The endurance required to stand in an operating room for twelve, fifteen, and more hours a day is only one of the physical challenges. The steadiness of hand and the fine-motor control needed by a brain surgeon—frequently working under a powerful microscope in order to make miniscule movements measured in tiny fractions of millimeters—are often the first physical skills to go as someone gets older.

While Ben felt confident the experience he brought to the operating table far outweighed the slightest changes he might have noticed in his physical abilities, for the sake of his patients, he decided to retire before any loss of surgical skill became an issue. "Better to give up the practice of surgery while I still knew I could go on," Ben explained, "than to wait until there was a noticeable decline in my abilities which could endanger my patients or prompt my colleagues to begin wondering whether or not I'd *needed* to step down."

It was not an easy or simple decision, because Ben knew it meant giving up that part of his profession he loved most and a role he felt God had specifically gifted him to do. "I realize it will be a major life change," he admitted to those who asked how he thought he'd handle the adjustment. "But I'm looking forward to not having to set my alarm hours before dawn in order to have the time I need to get ready for my day, drive an hour to the hospital, and get scrubbed in for a 7:00 a.m. operation that could last all day or longer."

The decision was also made easier knowing he wasn't retiring from medicine altogether. "I'll keep an office at Johns Hopkins where I'll still see patients, consult on difficult cases, and continue to teach at the medical school," he explained. "But I'll have more hours in my days, which is good. Because there are still many other things I want to do in the remaining years of my life!"

At the top of his post-partial-retirement agenda was Ben's dream of expanding the Carson Scholars organization he and Candy started in the 1990s. "Because we've been giving out scholarships for twenty years now," Ben reports, "we frequently cross paths with former recipients who make themselves known and want to thank us.

"Not long ago, I attended a Carson Scholars Award banquet in Pennsylvania where the emcee for the evening was a popular television news anchor in Pittsburgh. She told us one of her bosses at the TV station had been a Carson Scholar. I recently met a Carson alumnus who is now a software engineer quickly moving up the ranks at Microsoft. And just as we were wrapping up this updated version of *Gifted Hands*, another former scholarship recipient, an impressive young man who had since graduated from Stanford Medical School, applied for and won a spot in our neurosurgical residency program at Johns Hopkins."

Ben continues, "Candy and I want to grow the scholarship program to the point that every school in the country participates. Hopefully I will live to see a nationwide network of at least 100,000 alumni — Carson Scholars all over America maturing into young adults who continue to develop and use their intellectual prowess while still demonstrating compassion and care for others. What a powerful leadership base that could provide for our nation!"

In addition to the scholarship program, Ben wants to expand a second facet of the Carson Scholars Fund: the Ben Carson Reading Project. Because of the difference a love of reading made in his life, Ben and Candy's dream is to provide funding and support for schools around the country to create special places in their school buildings for children to read.

"School libraries are a vital part of most schools," Ben explains. "But students usually only go to the library with their classes once or twice a week for a limited, specific, scheduled time. And much of kids' time in school libraries is spent learning how to use the library (which is important), improving computer skills, or doing research for other classroom assignments."

So as this biography you are reading goes to press, the Carson Scholars Fund has already given nearly a million dollars to create Carson Reading Rooms at eighty-five schools in twelve states and counting—all dedicated to combating illiteracy and promoting leisure reading as a key to unlocking a child's potential. Decorated with attractive, eye-catching artwork based on Ben's "THINK BIG" philosophy, each room is filled with hundreds of books for students to explore from a variety of authors, topics, and genres.

The cozy environment encourages students and families together to recognize the importance of reading for leisure, learning, and fun. The Carsons' reading project began seeing results almost immediately. In 2012, students logged over fifteen million minutes of independent reading in the Ben Carson Reading Rooms. Teachers and administrators report this program "nurtures our entire school and allows our students to develop the skills necessary to become lifetime readers and learners."

According to Ben, "That's the whole idea behind the program. As more kids in more schools find out reading can be fun, I'm confident that discovery will change their lives like it changed mine."

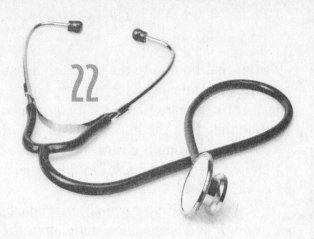

A Challenge to Young Americans

In 2012, Ben and Candy wrote a book together for the first time—*America the Beautiful: Rediscovering What Made This Nation Great*. While they had written this bestseller mostly for an adult audience, many of the issues addressed were things Ben felt he also needed to be saying to teenagers and younger kids, which served to give him a major head start on some other plans he had for the rest of his life.

For twenty years or more, Ben had already been speaking once or twice a week to a wide variety of audiences around the country, sometimes around the world. He expected to do even more public speaking after his retirement, especially to younger audiences—particularly in the educational arena.

By the time *America the Beautiful* came off the presses, Ben had already begun incorporating many of his ideas from that book into the speeches he gave at schools to younger audiences.

For example, Ben says, "Young people today need to realize that the importance of and the emphasis on education brought a new, upstart of a nation like the United States of America to the leadership of the world so rapidly.

"And yet, if you compare standardized test scores in math and science for students in the most modern, technologically advanced countries in the world today, American students average near the bottom of the rankings. Kids, as well as adults, need to be concerned that we're fast losing our drive for excellence in education in our nation.

"I regularly remind young audiences," Ben says, "that the average American today lives to about eighty years of age. 'Which means,' I tell them, 'most of you have the first twenty to twenty-five years to prepare for the rest of your life. If you do prepare, and prepare well, you will have sixty years, perhaps even more, to reap the benefits. And if you don't prepare, you spend the rest of your life being one of the occupiers—who just takes up space without ever using his or her incredible God-given brainpower and abilities to contribute and make the world a better place. If you're able to read this book, you have that choice. But you have to make your decision early in life. This means taking responsibility for your own life and actions now—while you are young—and not expecting the rest of your life to be handed to you on a silver platter.'"

"The same thing is true in the civic life of our nation," Ben says. "Most adults (and it's even more true of young people) pay little or no attention to what's happening in Washington, D.C.; in our state capitals; or even in their local city or county government. I am no longer shocked (though I'm more and more concerned) when I visit schools and meet many students who don't know the names of their mayor, their senators and congressmen, and sometimes not even the name of the vice president of the United States.

"Which," Ben continues, "leads me to another concern I have for our nation today. As a people, we are becoming less self-reliant, less willing to exercise our abilities, resources, and rights (of life, liberty, and the pursuit of happiness) granted to us all by our Creator. And more reliant on others, especially on the same government that we know less and less about. Which is not the attitude or the spirit that made America a great nation!

"So I want to spend the rest of my life helping young people recognize what great opportunities still exist in this country. Never in the history of the world has a generation of young people had so much wealth, so many physical and educational resources, such easy access to so much information on any subject imaginable.

"The potential for young people to make a difference in the world today is greater than it has ever been. Which is why I tell them, 'Take responsibility for your own life, for your own education if you need to. You can go to your school library, your public library. Surf the web responsibly, and you can educate yourself in any subject you choose.'

"If you're having trouble with algebra or trigonometry or calculus, they have chat rooms for all those online. Say you don't understand the difference between a sign and a cosign—there will be lots of people in that chat room who will be glad to help. Not everyone learns or understands a subject in the same way. But if you keep looking, chances are good you will find someone who can explain it in a way you *can* understand. I learned what I needed to know by reading books from the library; that is still a good strategy. But young people today have access to so much more information in so many more places than I did. There is no excuse for not using the incredible resources you have!"

(Ben says he's always careful when he challenges kids to use the internet and to make use of chat rooms, that it's important to let parents know what you're doing. They can even be there when you're surfing and exploring new territory on the web.)

One reason Ben plans to invest so much of the rest of his life speaking to young people is because he has such high hopes for them. "I see the unlimited, untapped potential in today's youth," he says. "Which is why I remind them that a lot of the people who founded this nation, brilliant and brave people who worked hard and risked much to make our nation great, were young people at the time—in their twenties and thirties and even younger. Nathan Hale, made famous by his dying declaration that his only regret was that he had but one life to give for his country, was seventeen years old at the time.

"There are other examples," Ben offers, "from the fields of science and math: When you see pictures of Nobel Prize winners, most of them look to be in their fifties, sixties, and seventies—men and women who have put in a lifetime of work. But when you read the details, you frequently learn their biggest, most crucial discoveries and developments which earned their awards and established the foundation and direction of their lifework, occurred much earlier in their careers. Often they were in their twenties or thirties and full of youthful energy and initial enthusiasm for their subjects.

"I tell kids, 'You don't have to wait to be old and gray to get involved as a citizen, to make a great scientific breakthrough, to assume leadership, to be an inspiring example to others, or to make a difference in the world. If you want America to be beautiful for your children and grandchildren, get involved now, be concerned about something more than the next tune playing on your iPod.'"

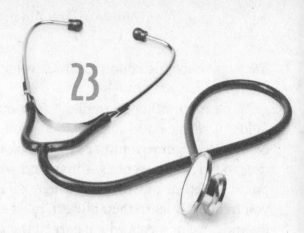

Thinking Bigger

Ben's retirement goal of making more speeches challenging young people and promoting his ideas from *America the Beautiful* got a surprise boost even before he gave up his surgical practice. In December of 2012, soon after he'd made his decision to retire, he was invited to give the keynote address at the upcoming National Prayer Breakfast. Although he'd spoken at the same event back in 1997, sixteen years before, the senators hosting the breakfast wrote inviting him to speak again. (The only other person to have done so twice was the 20th century's most famous Christian evangelist, Billy Graham.) They said in their letter that "this is a crucial season in our country and the world" with "a very difficult climate on Capitol Hill." They also referenced recent tragic events in Connecticut (where just days before, a terrible school shooting had left twenty-six dead, including twenty first-grade students).

The senators told Ben they believed all these things "highlighted a need for our nation to look to Jesus."

So Ben said yes to the invitation. He considered the opportunity not just a tremendous honor, but also a heavy responsibility—to once again address most of the leaders in the United States government and many world leaders all at one time in one place. He prayed as he always did when preparing a speech—asking God what he should do and say on such an important occasion.

On February 7, 2012, the senator who introduced him at the National Prayer Breakfast told the audience that Ben had been invited to speak "for three reasons: he loves Jesus, he has a compelling life story, and he is a distinguished man of science and healing. So we hope he can help us sort some things out."

After acknowledging the President, the Vice President, the First Lady, and all the distinguished guests, whom Ben said "included everybody," Ben first read four Bible texts he said would provide the context for what he wanted to say:

Proverbs 11:9—"With his mouth the godless destroys his neighbor, but through knowledge the righteous escape."

Proverbs 11:12—"A man who lacks judgment derides his neighbor, but a man of understanding holds his tongue."

Proverbs 11:25—"A generous man will prosper; he who refreshes others will himself be refreshed."

2 Chronicles 7:14—"If my people, who are called by my name, will humble themselves and pray and seek my

face and turn from their wicked ways, then will I hear from heaven and will forgive their sin and will heal their land."

Ben then began his remarks by saying he didn't want to offend anyone, but that he'd learned it had become hard to speak to any large group in America today without someone becoming offended. So many people wear their feelings on their sleeves and take personal offense whenever they hear someone say something they disagree with.

Ben said he believed such hypersensitivity is a serious problem today. Ben told his audience of political leaders that the modern concept of a *politically correct* speech makes people afraid to say what they think. It keeps us from listening to and learning from one another. It not only weakens us as a nation because it discourages the free exchange of ideas, but it robs us of one of our most essential rights — our freedom of speech.

He then shared some of his own personal story. How he'd been raised in poverty by a single mother who knew and taught her sons that the way out of poverty was through education. How she'd refused to see herself as a victim. How she worked hard, made no excuses, and refused to let her two boys make excuses.

If they tried, she would always ask them, "Do you have a brain?" And when they said yes, she would insist, "Then you have what you need to come up with a solution to your problems."

Ben went on to talk briefly about several other themes from his book *America the Beautiful*. He touched on some of the same themes and messages he shares when he talks to young people and children, starting with the sad state of education in our country.

Ben told his audience he knew some of them might be wondering why a doctor would think he ought to speak out about the serious issues America faces today. He suggested they needed to know, or remember, that five doctors had signed the Declaration of Independence. Doctors and educated people from all walks of life were intimately involved with the foundation of our country. And Ben suggested it was the nation's loss that the majority of those leading America today were lawyers.

When his audience of lawyers laughed (perhaps a little self-consciously), he explained what he meant: in law school, lawyers learn to *win*—to defeat their opponents "by hook or crook." Ben suggested our country and her government would be better off if all the leaders in the opposing parties in Washington changed their win-at-all-cost attitudes and began working together to solve the most serious problems facing our nation today. (The outburst of applause in response to that comment seemed to indicate there were a lot of non-lawyers present, and maybe even some lawyers who agreed.)

When Ben told that prayer-breakfast crowd his role model was Jesus, he received some more applause. And since Jesus told a lot of parables, Ben said he enjoyed telling parables and wanted to share one of his own—about a family with financial problems who tried a variety of "solutions" that made no practical sense, didn't work, and created serious conflict within the family. What

Ben's parable didn't say, because he didn't have to say it, was that the collection of faulty "solutions" that family in the parable came up with sounded a lot like our government's approach to its current financial crisis and federal budget problems.

He quickly addressed a number of other national issues directly. It might not have seemed politically correct (or at least not politically *smart*). But Ben called the country's debt a serious "moral" issue — in a room full of political leaders (of both major parties) primarily responsible for putting the country in such a deep financial hole. They'd proposed programs and then voted to fund them by spending trillions of dollars America doesn't have, leaving the mind-boggling bill for today's children and grandchildren to have to pay sometime in the future.

Next, Ben told an audience responsible for writing the tax laws and administering those laws that the United States' tax code is so complicated and poorly designed that no one can understand it well enough to be absolutely certain they are obeying it and not somehow breaking the law.

Ben told our nation's leaders at that prayer breakfast that he believed it was time to get rid of our unwieldy and unfair tax system once and for all. And he made a surprising suggestion about how he thought it could be done.

He explained that when he opened his Bible he saw that the fairest Being in the universe (God) had a revenue-raising plan for his people called a tithe. Ben went on to point out, "God didn't say if your crops fail this year you don't owe anything; nor did he say if you have a bumper crop you pay three times as much." The Jewish people were expected to give God 10 percent of their income.

Ben said the actual percentage of a tax might be different, but he thought the biblical principle of proportion would work as well for America as it had for the Jews in the Old Testament. Not only could it provide the necessary revenue in a fairer and more efficient way, but it would give everyone, rich and poor, a personal stake in the government.

From that point, Ben moved on to a politically controversial subject that impacted everyone in his audience: America's health care system. As a doctor he had some specific suggestions, ideas that seemed in direct opposition to the major revision of health care policy proposed and pushed by the president (who was listening intently just six feet away) and then passed by Congress (most of whom were seated at their breakfast tables right in front of Ben and scattered throughout the huge ballroom).

Ben hurried on to assure his distinguished audience that despite the serious and incredibly complex problems and divisive issues our nation faces today, he saw great reason for hope. He reminded America's leaders to consider our beautiful and inspiring national symbol, the bald eagle, and suggested we all need to remember that an eagle can only soar high and fly forward if it has a left wing and a right wing working together. At that point, Ben paused and smiled out over that crowd of thousands, almost equally divided into Democrats and

Republicans. As their laughter and applause died down, he added, "Enough said."

Another reason for hope he cited was his belief in a Creator who had given us all brains powerful enough to solve all the problems facing us today. And then Ben began to wrap up his remarks by retelling the familiar story of the "Star Spangled Banner," our national anthem, which was written about little Fort McHenry's improbable defense of Baltimore Harbor against the invasion by the entire British fleet during the War of 1812. Ben talked about what hope that tattered and torn Stars and Stripes symbolized in the dawn's early light.

His implication for the National Prayer Breakfast was clear. No matter the size of the challenges America faces today, if we use the tremendous brains our Creator gave us, and work and stand together instead of taking offense and fighting each other, we can once again be, in the final words of his speech, "one nation, under God, indivisible, with liberty and justice for all."

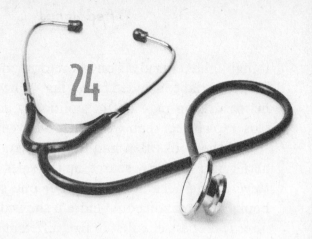

The Next Chapter

The response to Ben's prayer breakfast speech was immediate and overwhelming. Some critics attacked him for giving an inappropriate, politically *incorrect* speech they argued was intended "to embarrass the president" and other leaders of our nation. Many other observers praised his courage for what they described as "speaking truth to power."

The video of that speech went viral on the internet. Millions of people watched it for themselves on YouTube and scores of other sites online. Newspapers and magazines across the country ran news articles and opinion columns about Ben and the speech he gave to America's leaders.

The *Wall Street Journal* ran an editorial titled "Ben Carson for President." It cited his warning about politically correct speech being a danger to our country. Plus it highlighted his ideas on tax reform and medical care. The editorial concluded by saying, "The Johns Hopkins neurosurgeon may not be politically correct, but he's closer to correct than we've heard in years."

All the books Ben had ever written or had written about him suddenly soared up the sales charts. *America the Beautiful* became the number one seller of all the books on Amazon.com before it showed up on the *New York Times* bestseller list in five different categories. The previous edition of this book you are now reading was the number one bestselling children's biography on Amazon for the better part of the month after his prayer breakfast speech.

In the following weeks, every television network and radio talk show in the country seemed to request an interview. Ben appeared on a number of national broadcasts, including one of the highest-rated cable talk shows where he was the only guest for an hour-long program. The host and a panel of experts spent the entire time asking Ben to share the story of his life and faith, and then to elaborate on his opinions and spell out his ideas for solving a wide range of challenges facing America today—from education to national debt, the economic crisis, taxation, health care, and more.

During another television program, he recounted the wisdom his mother received when she prayed for God's help in knowing what to do with her sons. Ben smiled as he explained to the interviewer that his mother had evidently been something of a prophet. Because when he and his brother complained over the rationing of their

TV viewing, "I remember her telling us, 'If you boys keep reading books, someday people will watch you on television.'" He chuckled, "And here I am."

Whenever reporters or interviewers asked about his motivation for making such a "controversial" speech, Ben assured them he had not intended to be controversial or to offend anyone by what he said. He explained he had prayed about what he should say as he always did before any speaking engagement. He was merely expressing his own views on the topics he felt God wanted him to address. He added that he did think our national leaders too often acted like third graders at recess—arguing and calling each other names instead of trying to work out their differences. And a national prayer breakfast seemed like a good time and place to call for an end to such childish behavior so everyone could come together and set about solving the country's problems.

It seemed every interviewer wanted to know more about Ben's plans for the future.

After speaking out about a variety of national issues and making such an unexpectedly huge splash in the national media, Ben was asked again and again if he was planning on running for political office. He quickly replied that he had no such plans, and that certainly was not the motivation for anything he had said in his prayer breakfast talk.

Ben almost always added that for years people had been encouraging him to run for office. But he'd never felt inclined to do so. Indeed, he had always believed it could prove a hindrance to the work he felt called to do.

He'd even told interviewers, "The moment I decide to run for political office, I lose half my audience."

He kept explaining that his retirement plans were to spend more time growing the work of his charities. He continued to believe he could have the most impact by encouraging and equipping young people who would become America's next generation of leaders, by challenging them to use their brains and all the other resources God had given them—to THINK BIG!

And when he did give up his surgical practice at the end of June 2013, that's just what Ben began concentrating on. However, as people kept asking him about running for office, he laughed and said, "God would probably have to grab me by the neck and drag me into politics." But he told them he'd learned in his life "never to say never. Because I always want to be willing to do whatever I believe God wants me to do."

In Ben Carson's mind, no one can ever *think bigger* than that!

Ben's Spiritual Advice to Readers

I hope this book challenges you and other readers in many ways—to pursue excellence in everything you do, to use the brain God gave you to prepare yourself to do something that helps others for the rest of your life. Set high goals for yourself. Read to begin developing a life-long habit of learning. THINK BIG! Seek God's plan for your life, then trust him and follow it.

Actually, there are a number of challenges I would give any young person wanting to grow and mature spiritually. I read the Bible and pray asking God's guidance in my life every day; if you do that, I believe it will make a huge difference in your life as well. Get involved in a local church where you can worship God and learn more about Jesus every week. Look for friends who share your faith and will encourage you to live it out in your daily life.

I believe this is all good advice that will make a positive difference in your life. But you've probably heard it all before.

So I want to add some important spiritual advice that I don't think kids often hear. And it's this:

Don't just read God's Word—talk to him in prayer, spend time in his house, and hang out with other people who love and follow him. If you want to get to know

God, you also need to use your brain to learn about him and search for him. Start by opening your eyes and looking around you at all the evidence of his character, his greatness, and his lordship that God has left in plain sight. Consider the brain—how amazingly complex it is, how much information it can store. Did you know if you learned one new fact per second, to fill and overflow your brain with information would take you over three million years? So you never have to worry about overloading your brain. What does that tell you about the God who created you and your incredible brain?

Take a walk outside on a starry night. Look up. See the millions and billions of stars, hanging up there in order, at just the right distance so their gravitational pull doesn't destroy us. And ask yourself: How did that happen? Was it just a big bang? And if it was a big bang, how did that happen? Was there no matter and suddenly there was matter—perfectly formed and organized— did it somehow happen just by chance?

Some people think the idea of God creating the universe is nothing more than a *fairy tale*. The idea that our intricately designed universe simply began by some cosmic accident, without a designer, without any purpose seems to me a far bigger *fairy tale*. As a scientist I see convincing evidence throughout creation that a Creator God not only created a carefully designed universe, but also created us, loves us, and has a wonderful plan for our lives.

And yet, the farther you go up the academic ladder in school, the more frequently students are challenged about their faith in God. It's considered—by many people in authority—naïve, even ignorant. Certainly not politically or scientifically correct. Intelligent, well-educated people, especially scientists, are not supposed to believe in God. We're supposed to think that this incredible, intricate mystery we call life—and an entire universe that supports and makes that life possible—just happened? That it all started without a Starter for no reason at all? That's a lot harder for me to believe than believing in God!

I just don't have that much faith. And those who do manage to believe in nothing have to ignore a lot of clues God has left all around us as evidence of his existence. How can anyone look at a flower and think such beauty just happened? Never mind the fact that the flower has no way to pollinate itself except for the bees, the butterflies, and all those other little things that supposedly didn't come along until millions of years after the flowers—according to the evolutionists.

So how did flowers reproduce for all those millions of years? They leave out that little question. There are many little questions like that that evolutionists don't even try to answer. That's because the only possible answers are these troublesome conclusions that don't fit their evolutionary theories.

But they fit beautifully into the paradigm of a loving Creator. And I'm convinced that's why God gave us our complex brains with these giant frontal lobes, so that we can observe, study, learn, and integrate all this information. And when we do, we find it all points to him because he wants us all to know and trust him.

Yes, he's given us a Bible to read. And we need to do that. But he's also given us eyes, ears, and a brain. And he laid out all of creation in front of us and all we have to do is look at it. In the same way studying the various works in an art gallery tells you about the artist or sculptor, studying various parts of creation can teach you about the character and intention and greatness of the Creator.

Many people consider scientific truth to be a threat to their faith in God. And for some people it is. But it shouldn't be because all Truth is God's Truth.

But to be a scientist who believes in God (and there are a lot more of those than most people realize), to understand how creation gives convincing evidence of a Creator, you first have to know what you're talking about. So when you get in biology class and hear the theory of evolution, don't think you need to argue with the teacher. Make sure you understand all the concepts you're being taught—such as *microevolution* and *natural selection*. Understand what those terms mean and don't mean. They mean *it is possible for changes to occur within species*. And there is scientific proof of that. But that doesn't prove the overall theory of evolution.

Microevolution and *natural selection* simply indicate God gave his creatures the ability to adapt to their environment, so that he didn't have to start over again every hundred years or so. It shows how wise and flexible God is—that he gave his creatures adaptability too.

But there is no evidence that one kind of creature, one species, ever evolved into an entirely different species.

There never has been any evidence found that proves that ever happened. It's all just a theory. Merely speculation that assumes if a species can slowly change and adapt over time, then surely one species can gradually evolve into other species over longer periods of time.

We can ask, "Why is there no evidence of that?" But we are told, "Because it takes such a long, long, long time."

And yet, if you look at earth's population, it raises another serious question. A graph of population growth starting with two human beings and multiplying to 6.5 billion (the world's current population) would stretch over a six-thousand-year period, not the half-million-year period evolutionists estimate.

There is just so much that doesn't add up, so much that you are going to have to take by faith to believe evolution is the explanation for how, when, and why we got here. So many little questions that can only be answered with conclusions that point to a supernatural Creator as the easiest explanation to believe.

In the amazing complexity and potential of the human brain, I see all the evidence I need to believe in God. But you can find evidence of him in whatever part of his creation you choose to study. You just have to make yourself aware, know enough about the scientific facts to interpret them, and determine the truth for yourself.

When you do that, you'll discover that the evidence of God's love and purpose, like the evidence of God himself, is all around you, wherever you are. Realizing that will strengthen your faith more than you can imagine.